Praise For The Book

Sohini Rohra's book 'Cancelled to Crowned' is a powerful exploration of resilience and personal growth. As both a Mrs. India Earth 2023 and a seasoned counselling psychologist, Rohra brings a unique perspective to her narrative. Her ability to share deeply personal experiences while drawing on her professional expertise makes this book a compelling read. Through Rohra's journey, readers are reminded of the transformative power of faith and perseverance.

– **Dr. Marshall Goldsmith** ***(Consultant Psychiatrist. Past president, Bombay Psychiatric Society)***

Sohini's memoir is a thrilling journey through life's ups and downs, filled with laughter and tears. As someone who loves making people smile, I've found that humour has a magical way of easing pain's grip. Sohini beautifully highlights how humour can be our best buddy when times get tough.

– **Maniesh Paul** ***(Indian Actor, Bollywood Anchor & Host)***

Sohini's memoir is a symphonic masterpiece, weaving together the melodies of pain, resilience and self-discovery.

– **Ehsaan Noorani** ***(Musician)***

AF516801

In 'Cancelled to Crowned', Sohini paints a vivid and emotional charged portrait of her journey, each chapter unfolding like a beautifully crafted scene. Her story is a poignant reminder that life's greatest challenges can often be the very catalyst for our most profound transformations.

– **Kunal Kohli** ***(Film Director)***

This book by a psychologist who has achieved success in both the field of psychology and beauty pageants in spite of facing challenges like a stammer, losing a beloved parent to cancer early in her life, dealing with post-partum depression, surrogacy and having a beloved uncle with cerebral palsy, requires a blend of admiration, encouragement and acknowledge of her unique journey is commendable.

In a world where stereotypes often confine individuals to predefined roles, Sohini defies categorisation. She is a testament to the power of resilience, determination and courage.

Her journey serves as an inspiration to all who have faced adversity, reminding us that our greatest strengths lie not in the absence of challenges, but in our ability to overcome them.

Through often humorous, sometimes painful sharing and insights, she navigates the complexities of the human mind. You will find wit, wisdom, insight and inspiration – whether you're seeking guidance on your own journey of self-discovery or simply looking for a source of encouragement.

'Cancelled to Crowned' will undoubtedly leave an indelible mark on your heart and mind.

– **Dr. Kersi Chavda** ***(Consultant Psychiatrist. Past president, Bombay Psychiatric Society)***

I have had the privilege of caring for Sohini as her doctor over many years. I have witnessed her growth and metamorphosis from being that shy and hesitant young woman to becoming this confident achiever and role model for so many.

This book she has so thoughtfully written is her personal and professional journey. It combines soul bearing real life experiences with her expertise as a practicing psychologist as also her crowning achievement, Mrs. India Earth 2023. The chapters are written in 3 sections. They skilfully cover her overcoming her personal struggles and grief, her work building her personal and professional life, her achieving her dreams and aspirations and her solutions for building self-worth and successful relationships in a quest for finding joy and happiness.

The book is replete with profound personal messages from Sohini. It will give readers perspective, understanding and strategies with the potential to transform their lives.

I wish for Sohini all success, peace, happiness and continues growth.

– **Dr. Nozer Sheriar** ***(Gynaecologist, Obstetrician and Author)***

The amazing journey of Sohini is an inspiration for all who have had to undergo humiliation, rebuke and leg pulling due to no fault of theirs. To overcome a stammer requires mammoth handwork and dedication which Sohini was able to do. Her life has been a constant chapter of challenges from which she has emerged in a shiny armour. As her Principal IN COLLEGE, I am indeed very proud of her and wish her all the best for this heart rendering book. Bless you dear.

– **Dr. Subhadra Anand** ***(Author, Former Principal of***

Rd National College, Former CEO of Save The Children India)

Sohini Rohra's book "Cancelled to Crowned" is a powerful testament to the resilience of the human spirit. In a world where societal pressures often dictate our worth, her journey of overcoming personal obstacles to find self-worth is inspiring.

The intersection between beauty and mental-wellbeing is often overlooked, but Sohini's candid storytelling sheds light on this important aspect. Her insights and practical advice on prioritising mental health are invaluable in today's fast-paced society.

Sohini's book is a call to action for individuals worldwide to prioritise their mental well-being and embrace authenticity.

– **Gautam Ganglani** ***(CEO, Right Selection Global – speakers, coaching, training & events in India & Gulf)***

Sohini Rohra's book is a testament to the transformative power of harmonizing reason with faith. Her journey of overcoming personal obstacles and discovering self-worth showcases the strength and resilience born from nurturing both intellect and spirituality. A great read for anyone seeking harmony in life.

– **Khurshed Batliwala** ***(Author / Speaker / Art of Living Teacher / Alternative Healer)***

CANCELLED *to* CROWNED

CANCELLED *to* CROWNED

SOHINI

EMBASSY BOOKS
www.embassybooks.in

First Edition 2024
Published in India by:
Embassy Book Distributors
120, Great Western Building, Maharashtra Chamber of Commerce Lane, Fort, Mumbai 400 023, India
Tel: (+9122) -30967415, 22819546
Email: info@embassybooks.in
www.embassybooks.in

ISBN: 978-81-19726-31-8

Cover photo by Abheet Gidwani

Illustrations by Palak Agarwal

Printed & bound in India by Repro India Ltd., Navi Mumbai

My dear Ma

Your light still shines on me from heaven. I am who I am today thanks to your unconditional love and wisdom. I miss you and will treasure you forever. I love you.

Yours always,

Sohini

Dedication

To my Spiritual Master
Sri Sri Ravishankarji.

Foreword

In a world that is constantly asking us to prove our own self-worth, Sohini Rohra's memoir is a powerful testament to the indomitable human spirit. Overcoming a debilitating stammer to conquer the pageant world by winning a coveted title, and through time, ultimately finding her own self-worth, Sohini's journey is an inspiring read for anyone struggling to overcome their own challenges and discover their inner strength.

In the captivating world of pageantry, where poise and grace often take centre stage, it's easy to overlook the battles fought behind the scenes – the battles not against competitors, but against our own minds. As a winner of Miss Universe, I can honestly relate to Sohini Rohra who knows this reality intimately. In this insightful book on mental health, Sohini opens up about her personal struggles and triumphs, shedding light on the often-overlooked intersection between beauty and mental wellbeing. Through her candid storytelling, she invites us to embrace vulnerability, challenge societal norms, and prioritise our mental health in a world that often prioritises perfection above all else.

Drawing from her own experiences, Sohini offers practical advice, heartfelt encouragement, and a reminder that true strength emanates from within. The book covers a vast spectrum of human emotions, supported by simple yet effective coping tools, and opens up a whole new world of self-reflection.

Through her vulnerability, tears, strength and humour, this book serves as a guiding light – a reminder that amidst the glittering façade of life, our greatest victories often lie in the courage to confront our inner demons and emerge stronger, more resilient, and unapologetically ourselves. It all lies within us.

Lara Dutta

Table of Contents

Preface

This is my story and I share it with a heart full of love and gratitude. I intend, through my vulnerability, to help you find your own inner power, to feel your own light, and bask in your golden glory. This is something that pain can never take away from you; it may cloud your light but it cannot banish it.

This book definitely has a long list of beauty secrets from a queen but these are my glorious secrets of life, connecting to my most authentic self and finding gold in the eye of the tornado. I reveal these to you with both humility and utmost pride, through a heart full of prayer that you heal and rest where you belong… in the SELF.

I take a deep dive into the ocean of my life. It's been heartbreaking, grubby, chaotic, filled with defeat and cancellation along with beauty, resurrection, courage and gold.

My life's journey has shaped me into who I am today. My crown is only symbolic of who I always was, a queen in her truest form. We are all born queens and kings of our own universe, we all have the capacity to experience our light and we all have the power to emit this golden light of the inner royalty that we innately possess. All it takes is the mere realisation that we have the ability to transcend from who we think we are to who we truly are.

Our inner royalty is so potent that it is unaffected by victimhood, cancellations, fears, self-doubt and so on. We are whole and complete inside out. It is through some terribly painful lessons that I pick up my pen to write to you and share my lessons from trials to triumph.

Your highness, sovereignty stems from within you and not from the crowing of the world around you.

Love,

Sohini

Story (Part 1)

Once upon a time, in the afterglow of a full moon night, in a kingdom bathed in golden light, a little princess was born. She radiated the light of the moon who birthed her. There was something very special about her. The wind whispered the news of her birth and the creatures of the woods celebrated her arrival. The word of the princess's arrival spread far and wide. Even the elders of the village were enchanted by her – they could never fully understand why. Her big brown eyes gazed upon the world with wonder. Her loving gaze seemed to draw out the hidden magic in all things.

As she grew, she spread joy everywhere she went. The princess became known for her ability to see beauty in the most unexpected places. To her, every creature was a marvel, and she could find rainbows hidden within the most ordinary of things. Her laughter carried a musical rhythm and it ignited a sense of peace in everyone she met. She would wander through the woods, finding joy in the rustling leaves, the glimmering streams, and the songs of birds.

Yet, despite the light she emitted and warmth she ignited in the world, this beautiful girl struggled with her voice. When she tried to speak, her words would tangle, twist, clutch on to her tongue and clamp up her throat. The broken rhythm of her verbal expression made others frown in impatience. The royal courtiers, with their practised smiles and whispered secrets, would chuckle behind their fluttering fans. "Such a shame," they murmured. "A princess so lovely, yet marred by such a flaw."

The purity of her heart and soul was not enough, the world around her was ruthless and confusing. She began to doubt herself.

The creatures of the forest never judged her. They completely accepted her and saw her beauty beyond her stutter. She would sit by the riverbank while her four-legged friends wandered close to her. Watching her reflection in the water, she often wondered why she could not express the beauty she saw so clearly. As the seasons passed and years flew by, she withdrew more and more, retreating into the silent corners of her mind. These corners were safe, and thoughts were free to flow, even though her voice remained trapped.

One day, as she sat beneath an ancient oak tree, a wanderer came upon her. He was a traveller who had seen many lands, with a heart that held many secrets. His eyes held the depth of great wisdom, he seemed like he was the keeper of the ultimate secret of life. The girl looked up at him, both startled and awestruck, but the kindness in his gaze eased her fears and brought a calmness to her soul. He sat beside her in silence, while she matched his silence and rested in his comfort for a while. They simply listened to the rustling of the leaves, the distant call of a wolf and the inner calling of stillness.

The wanderer finally asked, "What is it that troubles you, my young one?" His voice was gentle and soft like the murmur of the stream.

The girl hesitated, then slowly felt safe enough to let her words tumble out. She told him of her struggle, of how her words failed her, and of how she felt that something inside her was broken. As she spoke, her heart began to re-open, the tears she had long held back began to fall, each one being drops of her sorrow.

The wanderer listened patiently, no confusion, no scowl and no chuckles. She felt a freedom while speaking and found her words flowing, not tumbling out. When she had finished, he placed a hand on her shoulder. "Do not mistake the silence within you for weakness," he said with a kind softness. "Inside you is a wellspring of wisdom, a voice that is as powerful as the winds that shape the mountains. This is not the voice of others; it is your own, waiting to be discovered, nurtured and heard."

From a satchel tucked across his shoulder, he pulled out a small worn book. "This is the beginning of your journey to discovering your voice. Take this book, and let it be a guide for your own journey."

The girl took the book with trembling hands, feeling the weight of the wisdom his words contained. As she opened it, the empty pages called out to her. It was as if the book itself was a living thing, waiting to breathe and evolve with her thoughts and experiences.

"Remember," the wanderer said as he stood to leave, "your voice is not something that can be measured by others. It is the expression of your soul, and it will find its way to the surface when you are ready. Until then, let the world be your ink, and your heart the pen."

The girl watched as the wanderer disappeared into the forest, the book clutched tightly in her hands. For the first time in a long while, she felt a spark of hope. She knew that her journey was just beginning – a journey of self-discovery, of finding her voice, and of sharing the beauty she saw with the world – as she put her first words on paper.

And so, the book of her life began, its first chapter written in the quiet of the forest, under the watchful eyes of the full moon that birthed her.

Stammering into My Fortune

Segregated Words, Integrated Heart

As a child, my home offered safety and comfort like that of a soft silk duvet wrapped around me on a cool winter morning. I would wake up every day by compelling my mother to cuddle up with me in bed and she would oblige each time – she would complain a little, but oblige. I so clearly remember the sweet smell of the kitchen that she carried on her nightdress as she allowed me to wrap my legs around her and squeeze her in my arms as I fell back to sleep in that unconditional comfort of her touch and smell. My mother and I had a bond that was both solid and fluid; she was my mother, my guide, my best friend and sometimes even my child. She would then run off back into the kitchen because she liked to micromanage what I ate as if my life depended on her packing my lunch.

I've never been a morning person, to an extent that I still struggle through my mornings. The only person who managed to get me out of my bed as a child was my handsome father. My dad would shock me with disturbingly cold, icy water and jolt me out of sleep. I don't know if it made me laugh or cry or whether I still miss my hearty mornings with my parents. But I do know that my parents' unique ways bring a smile to my face even today as I recall my mornings as a school-going girl.

My most precious gift as a child was my full house. It was a warm, cosy, colourful casa with my parents, my brother, my nani (maternal grandmom), my mama (mum's brother), my masi (mum's sister) and her two beautiful children. I grew up feeling accepted in the safety net that my home offered me as compared to the cold ruthlessness and rejection that came from the outside world. Life outside my home was like going to war every day – a battle within myself and a battle within my environment. The children in my neighbourhood were cruel. Growing minds are still learning but the trauma of hearing their "ttttttt… kkkkkk... ppppppp" followed by their vicious laughter still lives in me today. I was ashamed of myself; I hated the loser I saw in the mirror every single day and wished that the earth would suck me in every time someone imitated me. I stammered so much that I couldn't even pronounce my own name.

There were some days when I just couldn't gather the strength to face the bullying. I would decide to sit by my window and watch the kids play instead. With a heavy heart I would fight the little girl inside of me. All she wanted was for me to embrace her and to set her free. But instead, I chose to stay in and act out the role of a teacher to my floor tiles. Looking back, my heart aches to think that the little girl had made peace with the idea that the one-by-one tiles in her room were her only friends and a safe space to not only be her authentic stammering self but also the powerful girl she aspired to be. So, I chose to bully the tiles instead.

My mind goes back to a time when I was 12 years old. My father would always give me a loving kiss on the cheek as I exited the car to head into school every morning.

The feel of his clean-shaven cheek and the fragrance of his spicy aftershave would stay back with me as the last bits of comfort and safety as I walked into the big bad world. Back hunched and shoulders slumped, I'd hold on to this withering fragrance of safety and breathe it in bit by bit hoping to get through my day.

My mother would give me two rupees to buy a snack from my canteen at school. My mouth waters as I think about that bread topped with delicious chana (chickpeas flavoured with Indian spices). Come to think of it, it probably does because I only dreamt about eating it and on rare occasions managed to get my hands on it. The canteen was in a small gap under a lemon-yellow stairwell behind a brown hand railing. Over 50 hungry girls pushed each other to get their hands on their favourite snack tucked under the narrow passage. I'd zip out of my classroom as soon as the snack-break bell rang and run as fast as I could to make it there first. But by the time I stuttered through my order, the spot would fill up, the pushing would begin and I'd go hungry. The snack lady eventually started handing over my favourite chana-bread wordlessly, if I was lucky enough to make it in time. But it made me feel inadequate, insufficient and incapable. I hated it when someone finished my incomplete thoughts, fuelling my lack of acceptance towards myself.

I decided to quit my trips to the cafeteria and save my money instead. I used to take the school bus home; it was a small green mini-van. But this mini-van was my biggest zone of skin-crawling self-shame. My self-worth got crushed every day, whatever little I'd manage to build through the day. Yet, at age 13, I discovered an escape! Largely escaping my own self-rejection, I'd save my money and ride the public bus home. Big red bus #211 was the big protector of my dignity and pride. I just had to cross the road, fight my way through the crowds as I squeezed in and prayed for a seat. Ride past a few roads and skip home through bubbles and rainbows, with the bullies now history. I had arrived safely, earned my pride and won my freedom.

But then came the dirty man.

The demon

A short grotesque man with pitted skin and a feeble moustache decided to make me his prey. He waited at the bus stop and closely watched me for a few days. Seeing me board the bus every day, he began stalking me. He started following me into the bus, following as I walked home, getting disgustingly close to whisper tasteless vulgarities and touch me inappropriately. One day, I found him standing under my home and piercing into me through his ugly beady eyes as he watched me bully my one-by-one tiles.

This continued for three years. The dirty man... I wished daily for him to die in his sleep. Why and how did he get so confident?! It was my lack of voice and low self-worth that fuelled the abuse, gave it strong courageous legs, the slithering touch and those evil perversive whispers that shamelessly tortured me for three years and haunted me for decades after. It was only when my dad found me standing at the public bus stop one day that I was rescued from this trauma. What was worse – the devil from the public bus or the bullies from the school? I finally lifted the weight off my delicate shoulders and voiced my three-year ordeal about how the empowering escape had quickly dropped me into the hands of the devil. My black box of dark secrets had been opened and finally there was an end. My father's expressions ranged from shock, to anger, to helplessness, to sadness and then to shock again. My mother's reaction sat on the big fat couch of self-blame and guilt. Storms of rage and protection rose in my home. Waves of turbulent emotions ran through all the members of my family. All they wanted to do was protect me, free me, help me find myself but that power lay with me.

The storm finally settled and the sun shone again. Their anger eased, wisdom arose, focus came back to the centre. The lioness set out to cure the root cause of the weight on her voiceless cub's shoulders. She had to find a cure for my stutter.

So, there is a GOD!

Speech therapy, pranayama, meditation and yoga had been

a consistent part of my life. My mum always believed that healing needed a holistic approach and I grew up watching her nurture her body, mind, intellect and soul. In my eyes, my mother was pristine. Her name was Pari, which means fairy. Skin flawless like creamy milk, big brown eyes, thin pink lips, petite, soft, kind and compassionate with a temper sitting on the tip of her little nose. Her heart oozed with abundant unconditional love for the world around her. She taught me to love but she couldn't teach me to love myself. All she knew was to give limitlessly. Loving and choosing myself is a lesson I've recently learnt.

This gorgeous lioness was on the prowl. Her cub was hurt. She was relentless, she knew how to go after what she wanted, and what she wanted this time was for her cub to find her strength. In a small Indian village, my mom found a stammering cure centre. I still recall my first day there – I was such a misfit and yet such a fit. We were seated in a circle among 20 people with speech issues. I was surrounded by stammering "replicas" of repulsive me. I squirmed as I watched them strain through the alphabet, distorted faces twisted around basic words.

My mother tried instilling in me the "superpower" of faith since I was a baby but, so far, God had only been theoretical. But that changed for me the very instant the therapist met my gaze. It was almost like he knew what I was missing and got my theories to life. "Do you order your heart to beat? Lungs to breathe? Stomach to digest?" He asked who runs the body. "God," I replied. He had a magical effect – I still don't know what it was – I still don't know how. I was born again that day, his magic changed my life.

My dad took me to that Godsent centre located in the slum far away. I let my body and mind do the exercises while my heart surrendered to the divine. What happened at that centre, I still don't know. But that man was the first angel I consciously encountered.

My speech started getting better, and with that my self-perception started improving, life started getting better and my hunt for my spiritual Guru began.

I've come to realise that faith is an essence of life and grace its better half. Yet, I find myself yearning with a self-absorbed desire to control life rather than receive its gifts. My fantasy lures me towards my grandiose dreams and tailored future, giving into my fears and fuelling my anxiety. The only success I find is in my disappointment as I down the bitter shot of despair and more anxiety. I simultaneously find myself wishing to live in the present moment and being greedy about soaking this sweet nectar. The choice lies within! It all comes down to breathing (pranayama), dhyana (meditation), the rational (practical), action and surrender.

Wisdom appears when the recipient is ready

I started actively seeking my Guru... I felt his presence – my heart told me he was out there. While I continued pursuing my studies, forming long-term friendships, and succeeding as a fashion model, my search never ceased. I explored multiple paths but never quite felt quite settled. Then in 2008, I discovered the Happiness Programme, breathwork and meditation formulated by the Art of Living.

I experienced my first Sudarshan Kriya. Hearing Guruji's voice guide our meditation with the mystical transcendental "SOHAM", I felt a new form of true bliss. I also cried with a strange pain pervading through my body and mind as I headed home afterwards. Overwhelming bliss coupled with suffering – unable to comprehend my experience, I fell quickly into exhausted sleep. Awaking the next morning, my face glowed as though the sun rose within me, and my pain had vanished. My mind now peaceful, silent and rooted in the present moment. And my heart – it had found that warm, cosy cove that I had lost while growing up. This time, it was within myself. I knew I belonged here. But the big task was pending – could I entrust my inner journey to this master? I needed to meet him.

The Guru

The inner bliss just drew me in. I didn't want to stop meditating. So, I decided to meet the Guru in person. In 2008, I flew to the Art of Living International Centre in Bangalore. After a one-and-half-hour flight and two-hour drive, there I was, still oblivious to the fact that I had found my home. At the entrance, we were greeted by the happiest security guards I'd ever seen. People at the reception also stood with smiles, joy, and patience. What was up? Were they on something? I decided to plaster a strange smile on my face to mask my suspicion.

My body began to relax almost like I was getting intoxicated, like the first hit of a glass of wine as it streams down your veins. I remember staring at a beautiful water body in the ashram. The water brought a coolness and yet a warmth in my entire being. It's been 17 years and I still struggle to describe the magic that sparks within when entering my refuge – the Art of Living International Centre. All I know is, I am home. The inner turbulence settles, the stress dissolves and I cross over into blissful surrender. Though my rational mind cannot grasp, it can somehow grab and embrace what transpires in my soul. I feel overpowered by a safety and belongingness that words cannot express.

Love at first sight

I was on a mission. My future Guru was about to be tested and I was all set to grade him. I entered focused with my checklist and my grade card in hand. The captivating ashram could not lure me into its beauty – I loved control too much to consciously surrender it. Awaiting his arrival in the lotus-like Vishalakshi mandap, I was on high alert. He entered, met my gaze, and all intentions melted, my mind went blank. Weeping unabashedly as a newborn in its mother's consoling arms, defences dropped in their entirety. My questioning mind dissolved into my fluttering heart. Like love at first sight, I was now being guided into realms beyond rational thought.

In his presence 17 years later, my heart still flutters, my soul still floats and tearful joy takes over. That day just remains so crystal clear – his meditation guiding me deep into my inner home, dancing unabashed in free surrender, surrendering simply to myself. Divine intoxication taking me skyward, face soaked with ecstatic tears and feeling closest to the person I was furthest from – ME. I needed to be alone now, uncertain whether this torrent was bursting with joy or sorrow – only that the divine had assumed control and I belonged.

Bhanu Ma, Guruji's sister, discovered me there – so broken yet so whole. With a mother's ethereal empathy, she embraced me in her warmth, whilst allowing me to undergo my transformation into profound rebirth.

I had found home, anchor, fuel, faith, family – my Guru. This marked simply the beginning; that blessed programme gifted me the means to uncover and sustain my own strength, peace, and purpose. I was broken down to reform, complete and boundless. Gratitude empowering me to give freely and receive abundantly as I emerged into the new me.

With grace and unconditional love, my Guru had set me free. I will be forever grateful to my teacher for facilitating that.

Some experiences are so mystical that they have no evidence of logic, whereas others are so logical that they make complete sense to the rational mind. Both these kinds of experiences are important and have a role to play in our life. Imagine constantly looking for evidence and proof and losing the gift of the present moment. Now, isn't that illogical?

I want to share one such mystical experience that doesn't make any sense while it still makes complete sense. It involved my Guruji.

I was five months pregnant in the last leg of 2009. My husband Hitesh and I went for a friend's wedding. I had a difficult pregnancy and we hoped a getaway would change my mental scenario.

But fevers and bad coughs took over as we arrived. It meant I stayed in bed and I felt so disappointed. With no appetite, I ate bland rice, random wedding snacks, just trying to get through each day while I stared at paradise from afar.

And then I came across the Indian kali dal makhani right in the midst of an island in Thailand. The homely spicy lentils warmed my soul, making me want to dance. Funny how comfort came from something so simple! That dal became a loyal friend, soothing my spirit when nothing else could.

Come to think of it, beauty is everywhere. All we have to do is look under our nose. Beauty lies in simple joys, not just grandiose adventures. I quietly rested through those modest bowls of dal and discovered my true love for this Indian soul-food in a country far away from home.

I swore off destination weddings for the next few months. I had learnt a precious lesson for life – when you feel low or disappointed, look around and you will find small delights, little pieces of joy that are decadent for the heart and soul. Like my warm bowl of soupy kali dal that I love to this day – my go-to cosy pot when I need soothing.

So, there I was, five months pregnant and completely miserable. I was on vacation; I was meant to feel better but got sick instead. I cried and cried, the migraines were bursting out of my skull, the nausea was constant and the fatigue was taking over more and more, day by day.

I was so angry at God. I was so angry at my husband, who had it easy, the unpregnant to-be parent. I was angry at life, period! I demanded proof, "Show yourself, Divine! Prove to me that you've got me and explain this suffering!"

A week passed. Hitesh committed us to a friend's wedding back home in Bangalore. He was bursting with excitement. Another wedding? I sulked hard but he insisted that it would be good for me. Before I knew it, we flew to India, not home but to another city in India, to attend yet another wedding.

In Bangalore, my mood lifted unexpectedly. Festive celebration, delicious food – or maybe it was just that endless spicy dal makhani I had now made my comfort food. I had just about started enjoying myself when Hitesh, the unpregnant to-be parent, announced that we had a long drive to the venue at 8 am the next morning. Cue, pregnancy hormone nuclear blast!

But then, during the angriest two hours of my life, we drove towards a familiar peak. "That's my Ashram!" I yelled in excitement. My spiritual home! There I was, pulling into my safest refuge, just what I needed. How did I even get here? Maybe God heard me after all.

Guruji himself would attend the wedding! I eagerly awaited his arrival, my inner child doing a dance inside of me and my heart fluttering as I longed to see his smile.

He arrived, glowing. I watched from afar, guarding my precious baby bump from the crowd. He waved at me and smiled as he called me closer. "Are you happy now?" he winked. "No need to fight, just ask." Then he gently breezed on, leaving me comfortably numb in his aura. In that perfect moment, resentment vanished into the inexplicable beauty of grace.

Concrete uncertainty – testing faith

Even after meeting my Guru and melting into the self, I discovered that inner life is constantly changing. The upheavals are still persistent and uncertainty is most definitely concrete.

There are cycles of lapses, followed by grace and inspiration. Moments into old habits, followed by willpower and discipline. Times of relentless faith and surrender, and moments of fear and anxiety. All of it being part of the whole, the whole being part of it all.

My mind goes back to that earth-shattering August day in 2017. My greatest fear came to life, unleashing violent tornadoes within. Tornadoes I could not withstand even if I tried. For all my struggles with numbers, seven lives on embedded in my soul, 7th August 2017, when I learnt of the monster eating into my mother's body – that forbidden "C" word.

The ruthless ambush

Cancer, the unwelcome intruder, ruthlessly ambushed into the night, stole away my peace and joy. It snuck through with stealth and then stripped my family bare, ambushed the throbbing heart of this unit and robbed us of sleep, drowning us in uncertainty and fear.

My mother – my pillar of strength, my most solid anchor through all my inner and outer turmoil, my source of confidence – was suddenly failing. This petite yet awe-inspiring woman who held our family together would soon herself come undone.

And I was lost, as my perfectly packaged notions of faith crumbled like a pack of feeble cards. I was so angry, the unknown forces I deeply trusted had abandoned me. They seemed cruel, incompetent and powerless but perhaps I was most enraged at my own powerlessness.

In her eyes I had experienced glimmers of the divine – pure unconditional love glowing despite the harsh everyday reminder of the impermanence of her current life. And the thought of losing this beacon, my source of light into the unknown, which now I did not trust, triggered a childlike helplessness – rage towards reality's ambush on my warm colourful cove, my little universe.

That diagnosis brought about a significant shift within me. Sadness clouded my life, disappointment and weakness drained me down to emptiness. I lost my sense of purpose while fear and anger tightly knotted the centre of my being.

Through those dark days, compassion fell away, for the self and for others. I looked at the world around me with blame and bitterness, projecting festering wounds upon all surrounding me.

With time and patience comes healing, and with healing comes clarity. And with clarity I came to understand that our outer emotional landscape more often than not reflects our inner terrain. When we harshly judge our secret dark places, we cannot turn our breakdowns into breakthroughs. It is in self-compassionate moments – where we meet our personal suffering with self-love – that we can illuminate our lives with growth and purpose.

Even an earth-shattering, life-altering diagnosis holds this profound power. By taking responsibility for our feelings, going beyond blaming the self or others, we can create a pathway for inner healing and liberation from trauma. The turmoil will come, the rage will emerge and fear will try to hold you back. But peace and healing are rooted in mindful inner work, in accepting the inner wounds with love and lack of judgement and watching them patiently heal like a mother watches a child.

I lost all my faith when I saw my mother wilting away in this tsunami that hit me in 2017. In spite of that, I still anchored myself in meditation and breathwork. Though I felt bitter towards my Guru, these gifts from him were my life rafts that saved me from drowning. I fought my Guru hard, but he never abandoned me. He kept blessing me unconditionally with gifts that helped me stay afloat and survive the wreckage each day. I was angry with him but continued to embrace his teachings and eventually those little rafts turned into gorgeous yachts in which I rest even today.

When we go down, we come up again

Six months before my mum passed, I was dry, fearful, fatigued and sucked deep into a dark void. My brother and I spent two worried nights together while she was severely ill. On the second night, I lay exhausted on the couch, still in the previous day's clothes. Sleep-deprived and afraid, exhaustion finally pulled me into sleep. Intense visions flooded in... I was surrounded by booming chanting growing louder with an enormous chorus resonating, "I AM HERE!" In my sleep I screamed along; it was blissful yet deafening, reverberating and electrifying. I could hear myself screaming but I couldn't snap out of it.

My brother's shaking arms brought me back to the room and I emerged out of the trance wide-eyed, heart beating rapidly, failing to explain the intensity of my overwhelming vivid dream.

Miraculous news arrived of my mother's recovery! She was feeling much better and had managed to bounce back. Grace finally showered me with kindness and brought my aching heart to rest.

I was still lost in my surreal experience and drifted to the window looking upwards, blinking at the bright sun. Hours ago, all I could see was darkness lurking around me. Tears streamed down my cheeks as looked to the heavens. We grow up believing that God resides high up in the heavens. The gardeners too stared up at the skies. Suddenly, I witnessed a bright red heart-shaped balloon descending from the clouds towards me. It came right through my window with a message, "I AM HERE" inscribed on it.

I overflow with love and gratitude whenever I glimpse the tattoo on my right arm marking that pivotal day. I rediscovered my faith yet again and got reminded of the larger unconditional force that is watching over our little selves. I made a promise to never abandon my faith, however dark the road ahead seems. I promised to receive every gift that life offers me fearlessly.

Through darkness he gave me light, through anger he showered me with love, through resentment he persisted and nurtured my growth with gentle wisdom. I'm forever grateful to my guiding light Sri Sri Ravi Shankar ji for never giving up, even when I lost my way.

We are not alone. The divine song that answered my cries of despair with healing chants embracing "I am here… I am here!" blossomed into a deep calm and revealed the mystic magic that goes beyond the rational, logical mind.

The happy marriage

The marriage between the rational and the spiritual is one of the most successful marriages I may have witnessed. It takes focus, discipline, courage and FAITH to go after one's dreams. Through my life's journey, failures, achievements and then some more, I find a beautiful graph of ups and downs. I also find that my anchor lies right where the rational and the spiritual marry. In my opinion, it is only this marriage that can lead to true healing and healthy coping mechanisms.

Both have their role to play and both are incomplete without each other. When life overwhelms us, rationality guides us to seek clarity. And the peace that spiritual practices provide create a clear space for the rationality to clearly direct us. They take turns through the ebb and flow of life.

When we embrace both, neither is one stuck in the intellect over-analysing the magical intricacies of life, nor is one stuck in a blissful bubble of spirituality using it as a form of escapism. It is a beautiful balance where both ends of the spectrum meet to serve you optimally.

Faith is a natural phenomenon. It is a function of our psychological nature. Belief is expansive in its most authentic nature. It is not restrictive: neither completely spiritual, philosophical nor is it illogical. It is faith that drives us to use rational coping tools in a disciplined way. It is faith in the facilitator that allows us to listen and follow instructions. It is faith in ourselves that gives us the strength to pick ourselves up and work towards our highest self. It is faith that motivates us to keep at it and stay disciplined. It is faith that holds our interpersonal relationships close. It is faith that provides this safety. It is faith that allows us to shut our eyes and surrender every night. It is faith that sends our little babies off to school in the big, bad world every day. It is faith that lets you take that plane and fly 40,000 feet over the ground in a vehicle that is small and insignificant compared with the magnitude of the planet. The more I say the less it is. Accept it or not… it is faith that fuels the rational.

Neither faith nor rationality alone bring wholeness. Life is full of mystical wonders and too much rationality without intuition may lose out on the beautiful scent that oozes from this magic. But a spirit left unguarded by rational flavour may float off into irrational thinking and get lost in the colours of what may not be real.

Considering my training as a psychologist and my spiritual practice, people often ask me the role faith and spirituality play in psychological theories and therapy.

I believe the rational is the overt force and the spiritual, covert. Like the mechanism of the car functions optimally when supported by the invisible magical forces of energy like motion, air-resistance, friction and so on, the rational rides movement while faith serves through inspiration. On the other hand, rationality brings direction and focus and faith bring fire. You see, both cannot be separated from the other. Their power lies between head and heart. It is the balance between the two where both ends of the spectrum meet to serve you better. When they work together, they are like one orb lit aglow.

For some people, faith comes naturally. It has to do with how our minds work. For me, it is my psychological and logical limitations when it comes to measurable evidence that make me more likely to believe in the invisible forces that glorify faith.

When the heart and mind dance, faith and logic align

Do you believe that your life is controlled by external forces, such as God, fate, the environment or other people, or is your life driven by internal forces, yourself? The concept of locus of control refers to the extent to which we feel a sense of agency towards our own life – our perception towards the underlying causes of the events in our lives. If we believe that our life is influenced by our own abilities, thoughts, beliefs, actions and choices then we have an internal locus of control, and if we believe that the main causes of the events in our life are driven by outside factors other than ourselves, we have an external locus of control.

Faith and spirituality are driven by the internal locus of control. Faith thrives on personal experiences of intuition, inner peace, protection and conviction – though sometimes one may find oneself trusting tangible evidence and external validation over our divine inner voice. I don't have enough tangible proof to show that God exists and that I feel so connected, but on the other hand, I have abundant proof about the existence of the divine and my connection to it. Our beliefs lead us to our path, both inside and outside. The moment I met Guruji, he facilitated an imperative journey, a journey within myself. I reached a place inside me that was holding on to shame, fear, self-doubt, pain, resentment, anger and so on. This self-awareness gave me hope, peace and alignment. Which in turn gave me strength and focus. I now needed to free myself of these massive boulders I was holding on to. Faith created the space while my reason helped me work through my blocks and trauma. Faith gives us peace. Faith gives us strength. We have the strength to get back up and work towards our best selves when we believe in ourselves. Faith is what drives us to keep going and follow through.

Faith and logic – birds of a feather

Is constantly seeking evidence truly rational? Or does extreme logical scrutiny searching for tangible evidence eat into the beauty of meaningful mystical experiences that are beyond the realm of logic – like love, attraction, trust, intuition and awe?

The core truth breaks open when we go against the perfectly structured package of logic. It is boundless, infinite and free. Is the authentic flavour of true wisdom truly irrational, even-handed and open-minded? The "perfectly rational" flips to "perfectly alive" and then flips back to "not so perfectly rational but yet so fully alive".

I think that is where 'the truth' may reside.

Diving into the self

1. Reflect on a challenging experience you faced that seemed overwhelming. Write about how you managed to get through it and what strategies helped you succeed.

2. Consider alternative approaches you could have taken to address the challenge and how these could have turned the situation to your advantage.

3. Re-examine this experience and explore how it contributed to your personal growth. Did it lead you to a more evolved version of yourself with a higher purpose?

4. Reflect on a previous achievement that once seemed unattainable. How did you achieve it, and what did you learn from that experience?

5. Identify the sources of support you received during this difficult time and take a moment to express gratitude for their help.

6. Compile a list of your mentors, spiritual guides, mental-health professionals, insightful friends and family members, and create a record of your support network.

7. How can you integrate self-care practices such as journalling, breathwork, meditation, prayer, and physical exercise into your daily routine?

8. Assess whether your life feels balanced across all key areas: emotional, mental, physical, spiritual, social, and professional.

9. List the areas where you're experiencing challenges and brainstorm ways to address these gaps.

10. Explore how you can harmonise your spiritual beliefs /

faith with your logical mind to better manage life's challenges and enhance your overall wellbeing.

The purest nectar of faith flows in that sweet spot between the head and the heart.

Drumming to the Beats

The Melodious Rhythm of Life

My uncle Riaz is the sweetest big baby I know. He shone like a star in my home. He was handsome, like royalty. His gorgeous features were like those of a prince. His bright eyes, perfectly defined nose and his magnetic smile would light up any room.

I must confess that Riaz has been one of the biggest personal influences in my life. This precious man has played a vital role in shaping me into who I am today. He was a courageous man who savoured the beauty of life and relished the present moment in spite of living with spastic cerebral palsy. Cerebral palsy is a neurological condition that can present itself as issues with muscle tone, posture and / or motor disorder caused by damage or abnormalities in the brain. He was wheelchair-bound, struggled with basic self-care activities, yet exhibited positivity, energy and laughter.

Riaz was my mother's brother and lived under the same roof. His physical limitations were no match to his love for himself. Neither did he, nor us, give any special treatment to his condition or express pity. He was full of confidence and happiness and that clearly came from feeling embraced, devoid of shame or rejection. We were proud of him, loved him unconditionally and simply helped matter-of-factly with his needs. There existed no awkwardness around Riaz; he was naturally included like all members of the family.

I cared for Riaz like a mother; that's how I was conditioned from the time I was a baby myself. He was the biggest, most cherished baby of our home. I have the sweetest memories of cuddling up with him on his single bed some afternoons. His stiff hands and folded fingers would wrap tightly around me, both of us giving each other unconditional comfort. Those moments left me wondering, who was mother and who was child! Riaz was not a victim. He was bold, confident, courageous, independent, resilient and full of empathy. His wisdom and core values are imbedded in me even today and show up with his grace and beauty through the journey of my life.

Later in my life, I realised that to love so unconditionally with complete inclusion and empathy, and to fight the personal need to rescue our loved ones, takes immense mental strength and wisdom. To be able to empower a person to find their own inner power and become the best versions of themselves by sitting back and patiently watching the graph move from failure to victory is true love. I now understand that my parents' resilient empathy towards my trauma came from my wise big baby. This allowed both Riaz and I to self-emerge into our most authentic selves.

His self-care activities like showering, moving between wheelchair and bed, brushing his teeth, eating, and shaving himself eventually became his personal achievements. The home protected his dignity by encouraging independence and providing just the right amount of support.

I loved spending time with Riaz. Our favourite bonding activity was playing salon. It would give me great joy leaving his feet tidy with trimmed nails through my expert childlike pedicures. And it would give him great pride to "boast" about my spectacular services through sounds and gestures to visitors in the lobby where he spent evenings. He was an artist and spent most of his time drawing and painting. The neighbours would be delighted to check his new creations as he displayed his artwork with pride. He was a self-trained artist despite his severe disability. Everybody loved Riaz. His childlike innocence coupled with his wisdom gave him a charm that few could resist.

He cackled when he laughed and his whole body, though terribly stiff, would surrender to his laughter which came bursting out of his heart. Those around him couldn't help but give in to that infectious laughter. He had this natural ability to evoke empathy and joy. Riaz's spirit was vibrant. He was warm and playful. He was like a gentle sage who fascinated people with his cheer, laughter and kind eyes, undeterred by his body stiffened by disability.

I hadn't noticed Riaz's artistic abilities until one day my mother pulled out all the books from my study and dumped them on my bed. She was furious at me for my disorganised mismanagement. As she scolded, Riaz watched the show with patience and calm from the dining room. He then wheeled himself into the room and firmly indicated to her to stop. As I sobbed, he rubbed my head with twisted fingers and looked at me with gentle warmth. This may have been the first time I saw the adult in him and I naturally gave in to the comforting parent. He took it upon himself to teach me how to manage my study and asked me to wheel him to his room. He pulled out all his drawing books and showed me how to set them in an organised fashion.

He was an extremely organised and disciplined man, his books perfectly labelled and stacked one over the other, art supplies compartmentalised, sorted paints and pencils neatly arranged. This is the first time I opened one of his books and I couldn't believe my eyes. I couldn't believe that he was capable of this kind of supreme art.

That was the day I discovered that my uncle is a shining star. Riaz couldn't speak words but he spoke like magic through his art.

I would like to credit myself as a person who is well-organised today. The uncle with disability, playing roles of both parent and child, parented the messy niece. He fought against his own physical constraints and taught me life lessons wordlessly through the modes of love and example.

Riaz walked his talk even though he couldn't talk the talk. We all have gifts to share, wisdom to impart and strength to thrive, irrespective of our condition.

Riaz found humour in most things. Often people with cerebral palsy can grow frustrated and express it through temper, which Riaz did too. But he had learnt to cover it with jokes and laughter. Humour became Riaz's primary coping tool. His humour not only uplifted him but also brought a cheer to the lives of everyone around him.

Coping through humour

As a psychologist, I know humour can be very healthy unless it's unkind. Humour helps us cope with problems. A good joke can calm nerves, reduce stress, worries and anxiety temporarily. Laughter has a healing power; it releases feel-good hormones that trigger feelings of pleasure and decrease pain. It builds stronger bonds and gives hope. Humour provides resilience and also breaks trauma bonds.

Riaz often used humour intuitively and that made him resilient. Humour in difficult situations can reframe perspectives to a more positive and hopeful outlook. It makes tense situations lighter so we feel calmer and less overwhelmed.

Humour has an exceptional ability to strengthen bonds through heart-to-heart connections. Shared moments of warmth and laughter foster a sense of unity, understanding and companionship.

But humour is unhelpful when we use it to escape from difficult emotions, or attack people viciously through our humour with the excuse of "just kidding". Sometimes we need to feel our feelings without making a joke and Riaz knew just where to draw the line. He knew when laughter helped and he knew when it needed to be felt.

He switched between being my playful innocent baby and a wise sage who taught me core life lessons – often within minutes! He never denied his struggle and, on most days, readily smiled through it.

Riaz appreciated discipline and was quite organised himself – meals structured, soup measured, broken rotis counted, vegetables perfectly mashed into a consistent pulp, clothes ironed, eyebrows combed, hair gelled back and neck perfumed. This was his daily ritual before he bounced into the world every day.

There was this one time I hadn't showered in two days and was hiding from the world as usual. I was watching the kids play and was getting sadder and sadder drowning in my own shame and darkness. As I pitied myself, I watched Riaz being wheeled around the building compound by a beautiful girl. They were both laughing and giggling happily. Riaz was unashamed and living joyfully while I was hiding unbathed in a dark room and wallowing in self-pity. He was out there on a beautiful evening, wind blowing through his hair, owning his reality, inclusive of the pain and the beauty, and relishing the present moment. It woke me.

I learnt that self-acceptance was such a core essential for survival and happiness. He went from a state of victim to victor just by fully owning himself and living life without judgement. It would be fair for me to say that I didn't only learn but imbibed within me that perspective shapes our reality more than conditions.

After that, I hid less, showed up more, primarily for myself, and continue to do so till this very day. I have learnt to thrive no matter what my perceived "limits" are.

White crown of courage – my mother's battle with beauty and the self

My mother was gorgeous: flawless bright skin, big beautiful eyes and soft pink lips. She always smelled like a bouquet of flowers. She was picture perfect, inside-out. Her tailor-made couture, Indian cotton suits, flawless makeup, oriental exotic fragrance, matching shoes, topped with her addictive laughter and electrifying temper, made her the most beautiful woman I had ever seen. "God really put you together with tender love and care, ma," I'd tease her. She would blush like a teenage girl and laugh her way out of the compliment. My mother gave unconditionally from her heart and she had an innate ability to draw people close effortlessly with her warmth and care.

My mum handled life with both grace and gratitude. She managed to maintain a calm composure even through the stresses of life. I admired her balance and her capacity to put people she cared for before her. I was in awe of my mother and hoped that I could someday walk the world wearing her shoes, mirroring her wisdom. I hoped I could capture her loving essence, carry forward her legacy, and nourish people and the world around me with kindness and singular focus just like her.

But mum did it best – the queen mother wearing the white crown of courage, keeping us safe under her wings as she lit the kingdom centrally with her light and love.

But this is how I saw my mum.

She saw herself differently. The truth is that my mother suffered from a skin condition called vitiligo – a condition causing skin discolouration and white patches. Eventually it spread fully across her body. She lacked self-confidence deep down due to the harsh beauty standards that she had to adhere to during her youth. She hid her wounds behind her ever-giving nature, go-getter drive and occasionally short temper. She felt grateful for any affection that she received and returned the love by over-extending herself. She couldn't bear to see people suffer. She was soft, gentle, and kind like a loving queen. My mother taught me to give but she couldn't teach me to love myself. This I learnt a little from my uncle Riaz and most of it through my own life's journey.

Perspective – my mother and I looked at ourselves and each other so differently. I hated everything about me. While mom redefined beauty on her own terms, I was struggling down a parallel road that lacked self-worth and was crowded with harsh criticisms and judgements. Both journeys messy but learning to love and accept the self.

I eventually witnessed my mother blossom through self-work. Her focus shifted from outward to inward. She nurtured personal growth, empowered herself to reclaim her worth that went beyond external validation. But the truth is, it took the big C to teach her that. My mother came completely into her own when she stood eye-to-eye with cancer. She stood up for her rights, set healthy boundaries and expressed herself unabashedly in the last chapter of her life. Her beauty transformed magnificently in my eyes and that's the mom I hold on to today.

Losing my mother is the most unfathomable pain I may have ever endured and still hurts deeply. But I feel so full of pride and comfort as I recall who mom became through that suffering – a self-accepting and self-loving fighter who stood up for herself against all odds.

That woman is my strength today. The grace and courage with which she rediscovered herself as she looked cancer in the eye guides me when I start doubting my worth or power today. She taught that though we cannot control what happens, our perception is our choice. It's liberating to learn that limitations can be treated as futile and my responses are a power I will always hold – the power of perspective.

Pragmatism and self-assurance – my brother's boon to me

My brother and I are just 16 months apart. He was my best friend growing up. I got lucky with my brother; his steadfast support especially during my speech struggles instilled confidence when the outside world frightened me.

He would patiently wait for me to finish my sentences. It gave me a sense of confidence that even the adults in my life couldn't give me at that time. He always had this very old soul, wise man energy about him, perhaps because he learnt to play adult in our household of warriors very early in life.

We leaned on one another but turned out to be two very different individuals. Our contrasting childhoods left him pragmatic, and me yearning for compassion. He has the power to assess most situations cleanly – "It is what it is," were the wise words on the tip of his tongue. I, on the other hand, went from unbounding compassion to finally developing balanced empathy through spiritual work and the study of human psychology.

When turmoil strikes, his pragmatic analytical brain quickly analyses possible solutions, while I dive into understanding the reasons behind the turmoil before I look for solutions. Our philosophies differ but we celebrate each other's perspective alike. I find that reaching out to each other is often enough to blend our approach to achieve balance.

Even today through the storms, I run to be sheltered by his wide rational shoulders. To receive a harsh reality check with his unique ability to give it with patience and empathy.

We need them both – the beauty lies in both approaches. The head, the heart and eventually the marriage of both perspectives. The journey of achieving this balance paves the way ahead.

My family, champion soldiers

Growing up in a house where I witnessed people close to me face tribulations in their lives has made me more compassionate and empathetic. It is because I witnessed and experienced suffering that I understand suffering, and my instinctive response from deep down is to take the pain away. But I can say this because of my immediate environment's approach to adversity. All the adults seemed to have a sense of inclusivity of the pain each one was going through; they were more solution-oriented and didn't victimise themselves or each other. They were empathetic towards themselves and others and seemed to have a self-assured pride because they were all achievers in their own eyes.

And this is what I grew up watching and learning. My father left his home in Delhi and started life from scratch by sleeping at the station alone in Mumbai for days until he managed to figure out a roof over his head, eventually becoming a successful man who left no stone unturned through our growing years. Even his narrative described the pain but also celebrated his achievements. I don't think he ever felt like or projected himself as a victim – only an achiever who overcame life's challenges.

The superpower of perspective

My gorgeous holistic home full of broken but happy people gave me a superpower.

This is the superpower of perspective.

Perspective is a superpower – it gives us the power of choice. How we see things and what we choose to do with what we see. Our views get clouded by our beliefs, our environment, ideologies, religion, culture, childhood experiences, social constructs, trauma and so on. This tinted lens colours our interpretation.

Adversity can break or strengthen us based on our perspective. With a solution-oriented healthy mindset focused on growth and topped with faith, one endures gracefully.

Victor not victim

Growth happens in a beautiful way when we mend our

hearts and heal our minds to repair our lives. And this healing occurs simply based on how we look at what has happened to us.

Sometimes we cope through resentment, anger and helplessness. But adversity can be reframed into a fuel that drives change if we are willing to change the lens. Inner work heals outer wounds.

We were a home that was filled with suffering but full of happiness and pride. Facing any adversity as a challenge to overcome taught us strength, resilience, compassion, self-love and the power of faith.

Unlocking the power of perspective:

• Breathwork and meditation can clear the mind to process feelings better and kickstart the psychological work needed for healing.

• Accept how you felt in the situation. Label the feelings. Express them to someone safe or record privately.

• Understand the experience event-by-event as it occurred. Dissociate the feelings from the facts of the event. Taking help from a neutral party might help. Try to understand what truly triggered these feelings. Seeing events as factual information along with self-awareness helps to give you a clear perspective.

• Identify learnings to help process unhelpful feelings and move forward. Discussing with someone can be helpful.

• A third person's perspective – such as a trusted advisor not emotionally invested in the situation – may help you view it from a fresh lens and strip away personal bias.

• Spend time with the less fortunate or those different from you to spark compassion and gratitude. While we are in complete acceptance of our own feelings, it can help us see things in a new light.

• Change of scenery helps to refresh one's outlook. Disconnect to reconnect might be helpful.

• Respect your evolution and understand that you stand to grow through what you go through.

The most authentic locus of our life's control lies only with us. It can never be taken away. How we choose to see things and respond to them is a strength we all possess.

And that, your highness, is your power of perspective… it sets you FREE.

Diving into the self

1. Reflect on someone in your life who has navigated hardships with remarkable resilience and dignity. What specific qualities or actions did they display?

2. What insights can you gain from their experience that might help you tackle your own challenges more effectively?

3. Do you think it is possible to foster personal growth and empathy over helplessness and resentment while facing adversity?

4. How might this be achieved?

5. When you face a tough situation, do you generally perceive it as an insurmountable barrier? If so, what factors contribute to this perception?

6. How confident are you in your ability to overcome

challenges? What factors influence this confidence?

7. Can you identify and differentiate between situations that seem beyond your control versus those you feel you can manage? How do these distinctions affect your response?

8. Do you believe that difficult situations can be used as an opportunity for growth and learning? Why or why not?

9. Is it possible for you to consciously reframe your perspective to uncover the hidden lessons and strengths within a challenge situation?

10. What strategies or methods could you employ to cultivate compassion for yourself and others during tough times?

The energy that burns through pain, holds the power to heal. This transition from victim to victor is just a turn along the same path.

Grief

Still Yet Turbulent

My dearest ma,

As I look at the beautiful forms of mother through these nine days of Navratri, memories of you have taken over me. My soul is yearning for you, my forehead for your warm white slender hands, my fingers for your soft hair and my ears to be called "Poochie". It suddenly hits me that you've left me. All it took was a blink of an eye and my future with you was gone. I look back at the last year of your life, and dark memories of pain, suffering, deterioration, and helplessness surround me like a charcoal-heavy, unshakeable cloud. All my failed attempts at easing your pain, easing my pain and my internal war seem to be memories written in stone for now. I wonder if you are okay and safe, are you watching me, feeling my pain, and listening to everything unsaid that I want to say to you? My heart still beats for you, still looks for you and still breaks every single time over and over again like a fresh experience every time the grief hits me reminding me that you left. Denial has become my closest friend. She helps me get through life and forget our recent past. She helps me stay sane and then fails me like a trickster when reality hits. I still reach out to her like a coward who doesn't even have the courage to see reality for what it is. But how can I come to terms, ma... You are DEAD. My biggest fear took form and took the life out of me.

What if you were still here with me, by my side sharing my world with me and allowing me to melt into your womb. Your comfort, your softness, your infectious laughter and innocence had an undying magic, momma. You just made it all seem so possible and then you just left me in the blink of an eye. You left me to fend for myself and work it all out without the luxury of slipping, without the luxury of failing... No ears to listen to me anymore, no arms to hold me, no eyes to look at me like no other beauty ever existed beyond me, and no one to call me out and fiercely fight back.

You just left me, ma... I blinked my eyes and you were gone. My days just go by and I don't know how, my pain has become me... it's made its home in every cell of my being... unshakeable. Sometimes I wonder if I'm even ready to let go of this pain, to let you go... What if you were still here with me, sharing my world and allowing me to feel safe. Your eyes, ma, they were home. I feel homeless, unheard, and abandoned. My feet have lost their grounding, my home has lost its roof and my soul is wandering with a heart that has been crushed with its pieces lost.

I am just wandering through my life, ma... You took my soul with you, ma, and I yearn for you... I yearn for me. Who am I? Who am I becoming? I look into my own eyes and I don't recognise the person I'm looking at. I blinked and I lost you... I lost me. I find joy in small pieces of my life but it's just so empty, so unsafe, like a home made of dry sunburnt hay, so fragile and baseless.

How, ma, how? How did you just go, ma? Why can't I let you go? This pain and emptiness have taken over and I just can't seem to let it go, to fill this void, to let you go and to let me die.

I remember looking at you and wanting to hold on to you so tight while I also wanted you to just urgently leave your rotting body. How could I have even asked you to stay, shared my dreadful fear and insecurity with you? I didn't even have the courage to tell you that I love you, ma, and I need you to stay... I need you so I can survive. Neither did I have the courage to tell you to leave. I sat there in a confused silence every day of my life with my words lost in my pain.

How could I have told you that you are the reason I swell my chest and take on the world, that I could jump from the highest cliff and I knew you would catch me without a miss? How could I have told you that I'm scared, ma, I'm going to be so alone without you and that your baby is dying with you as she watches you fight with death every single day of your life? I wanted to beg you to give in to your death and I wanted to beg you to fight for your life.

How could I have expressed myself, ma? How could I have courageously looked into your eyes and hugged you without crushing my own soul knowing that it's not going to be okay, I am not going to be okay and that I'm dying along with you? I was facing my own death as I watched you slowly inch closer to your death every day, like slow poison.

What do I do with this empty space? I'm so scared to allow the pain to slip away. What if you were here with me sharing my world with me? Keeping it warm, cosy, flowing and filled with your big bright eyes, your laughter, and your innocence. I feel so cheated... why were you taken away from me? Why? Why did I have to watch you deteriorate so powerlessly?

Your grace, your beauty, your courage, your soft and infinitely large heart fit the entire universe in it. Your heart was so open and full it almost made me jealous and competitive. It was this beauty that charmed everyone who even got a glimpse of you. Your laughter still rings in my ears, my body craves your touch and my soul your womb. I remember looking at your ears as you were shrinking into the fragility that was taking over you and wanting to say so much. It all went unsaid, ma. I love you, my mumma. I didn't even know that missing could be so enormously painful, nothing like I have ever experienced before. The void like a bottomless pit in which I'm slowly freefalling into black doom.

But I also feel this strange unbeatable strength like I've never felt before. This feeling is of a serene lioness with a crown whose force and stability are deeply rooted and supported. I know my strength and I also know this time I cannot be shaken. My strength is untamed and extending intensely within and silent. My power comes with a fragility but it is this untainted frailty that is aligning me, making me more and more tenacious with every passing day. I want to welcome this transition but I'm so scared I'll lose you along the way. Help me change this fear, ma, include this malleable emptiness and allow it to do its job of toughening me... Help me make you my strength, ma, and develop the courage to become the person I'm becoming without you. I need to survive... I want to survive as my best version. Not your version of me, just me.

I want to allow myself to become again. I allow myself to grieve my own death. I'm allowing myself to rise again and be born again. I embrace the vulnerability that comes with my new birth and I accept this grief. I'm choosing not to evade this pain and I'm choosing to embrace my resurrection. I'm choosing to allow my tears and I'm choosing to embrace the vulnerability. I'm choosing to accept the anger and embrace the peaceful silence that comes with this acceptance. I'm choosing to let go of denial with love and gratitude for helping me survive and holding me strong when I needed her.

Thank you, ma, for being you, the best version of yourself, and giving me YOU so selflessly and abundantly my whole life. As I place you in my heart, I consciously free you and I from this bondage of our attachment and accept that our paths are no more the same. Our journey together was the most beautiful it could've been as I was blessed with grace personified to bring me into this realm and prepare me for my journey in this world. The time has come for me to take charge of me, walk my own path, leave my own footprints, and become the ocean I'm meant to be.

I bid you goodbye, mumma, with an empty heart, an empty soul, and a trembling body.

As my heart anxiously races, my mind resists, and my body fights me hard and strong, I bid you goodbye too, "Poochie", as you RIP in the warm secure womb of ma.

I love you my ma, I love you Poochie... my heart is your abode. Thank you... it was a RICH journey. Farewell, for now.

Yours always,

Sohini

An intimate letter I wrote to my mother and to my inner child — her dependent baby. I was overridden with a dark void one grief-stricken night, overwhelmed by loss and I took recourse in reconnecting with my mother.

Months had passed since losing my mother to cancer. I found myself perpetually at war with my grief. I oscillated between hyper function and extreme dysfunction. Fits of ceaseless activity to cope through distraction and utter shutdowns when the storms of sadness took over.

I often suppressed my feelings, pushed them deep inside me. I worried that if I let the feelings out, this heart-crushing void would show up my vulnerability and would paralyse me. I was afraid it would leave my raw vulnerability exposed, wounded and shaking.

This illusion of safety protected me, at least for a short while. It spared me from the shock, heartache and grief that I had already battled with for years. Through those years, I helplessly anticipated my mum's passing as I watched her body succumb to the suffering caused by the big C. I had to protect myself from my deep, dark and scary emotions leaving my mind clouded by suppressed grief. I was in denial; I would get out of bed after spending lifeless days just lying there, and resume life as if all was well. Nevertheless, the grey foggy cloud of suppressed hidden emotions ceaselessly left my days raining with sadness, guilt, shame, blame and a dysfunctional lethargic body. This veil was occasionally pierced by the sheer force of anguish, leading to a complete systemic collapse. Turbulent showers of loss would burst out of me as I lay like a corpse myself, mind screaming loud and my body unresponsive.

My fear about mourning openly made me adopt the unhealthiest approach possible. But emotions we repress and hide from refuse to be silenced; they creep up from behind, invisible like ghosts, and persist until you're forced to finally face the painful reality of what truly is.

I tried hard to create an alternate reality and numb my pain through dismissal. But there was no escaping the truth of my biggest irreversible loss. There is no release besides truly feeling what is. What we hide or run away from eventually comes and stands in front of us like a big monster... there is no escape.

Until we confront it and feel to release it.

Grieving can be exhausting. It had permeated my body, draining me of energy over the years. My body felt tired and frail at all times. My appetite was erratic, my immune system weak and my mind clouded. But no one could really see through me or understand what was going on. I was often praised for accepting my acute loss with poise, but inside I was tender, broken, fragmented and in need of immediate help.

Losing mom also stirs an undertone of relief, relief that she is free from suffering and relief from my daily anxiety of whether she is going to make it to the next day or not. But then this relief ignites guilt over its mere existence – relief? How could I be relieved about losing my mother? My anger reignites at this self-betrayal, which spirals me into blame and then guilt and eventually numbness again, leading to an endless whirlpool of extremely intense emotions, difficult for me to confront head-on.

So, I retreated into numbness to escape the pain. I found myself hiding from my grief because I lacked a safe space to dive into, vulnerable and exposed. To be able to safely process the pain and feel accepted with the rawness that came from my wounded heart and soul.

I oscillated between raw anguish and numbness, unable to fully face my pain. I was prepared for my mother's death; I knew it was coming. I pre-grieved for months on end anticipating her passing. But her loss left me devastated, my grief even more intense.

Still too overwhelming to immerse in it completely, I only dipped by toes into its shallow depths briefly before resurfacing. Avoiding it all costs, being pulled fully into its darkness. My extravagant pretentiousness elegantly hid this truth – my entire being longed to heal, to feel free and light again. Yet I remained too afraid of the intensity that this level of healing demanded. So, I floated at the surface, hovered in limbo and permitted myself only topical glimpses into the storm churning within.

My grief is long, deep and heart-wrenching but it is not complicated prolonged grief manifesting in depression. What I experienced is the regular cycle of grief. I anticipated my mother's passing for months on end but a loss is a loss after all. In complicated grief, coming to terms with the loss is very difficult, the thoughts are negative and dark. There is also an unmanageable confusion, overwhelming sadness, prolonged denial, erratic behaviours and a deep, dark void that creates an irrational longing for the past. Happiness seems impossible with a heavy hopeless emptiness making the future look bleak. My grief follows a natural course where full healing comes only when one finds the courage to face the pain. If one is experiencing complex grief, it is imperative to take support through the healing process. Healing is possible and the light awaits you.

In the eye of the storm

Coping with grief can be exhausting. It is exhausting to stay in the state of grief and it is as exhausting to help oneself out of it. How do I silent my mum's whispers as she was my alter ego? How do I not think of her because she was the voice that guided me through confusion? How do I not crave for her touch because her warm hands, comforting eyes and smiling face told me that everything was going to be okay?

For a long, long time, I caught myself dialling her number to share some minute victory or petty crisis, as I always did to hear her unwavering validation. But now there's silence at the other end of that line; her caring ears, loving voice and open heart have been buried with her fading form.

I yearn for her gentle touch. Her warm hands, comforting eyes and smiling face made it all okay. Her empathetic authority and strong will steered me in the right direction. Without her grounding presence, what reassurance remains that things will be okay when storms rage?

But no storms last forever.

This I can safely say is the everyday story of my life… some days bad and some days good but it gets better… it feels lighter. I found myself very slowly moving from the dark memories of how she wilted and faded away to now seeing healthy beautiful images of her in my head along with happy memories from the past.

The piercing pain began depleting and slowly started fading. Bittersweet memories surfaced and took me from darkness into her golden light again. The present still holds an inconsolable void but this void is full of her. Embodied by her glowing pride, her safe advice, her comforting touch – powerfully seated within. Intangible but felt deep within.

My sorrow runs bone-deep when memories assail me.

Though I long physically for the comfort of mom's soothing presence, the rational part of my mind does not split reality from acceptance. I can conceptualise happiness ahead, believing that, in time, this void will heal.

And then we're all okay

Navigating the deep and profound journey of loss is challenging. It is a transformative experience that requires holistic nurturing – the mind, body, and soul. A strong spiritual foundation, unwavering faith, and the ability to surrender were no match for the overwhelming grief of losing my mother to cancer. It left me completely broken and undone. I became more and more dysfunctional and vulnerable. I recognised the need for additional support and made the decision to seek help through grief therapy and medication to get my back into function. I realised I needed the strength to feel my feelings and process my pain.

It's important to understand that there is no shame in reaching out for assistance during trying times. We need to allow ourselves a safe space where we can be vulnerable yet feel supported while we face our demons of pain and loss. It can help us embrace healthy coping mechanisms that can anchor us and aid survival during trying times. Sometimes we all need a little hand-holding.

Seeking professional help, whether through counselling or medication, breathwork or meditation, nutrition or exercise, or a combination of all, is a sign of strength and self-awareness. It is a commitment to our own wellbeing and a willingness to take the necessary steps towards healing, resilience and happiness.

Healthy coping mechanisms, like a strong support system, listening to music, accepting our feelings and speaking them out loud, journalling, taking a short break or even spending time alone, can help us connect with ourselves and feel more rooted.

The path to healing is a subjective and non-linear journey. It requires patience, self-compassion and an open heart. By daily asking myself, "What do I most need right now?" and tenderly reaching out for it, I prioritise self-care, honour my uniqueness and take one day at a time.

I learnt to balance my grief by playing with my narrative. I reached out to sweet memories, started celebrating milestones, reminisced over photographs and began infusing myself with my mother's enduring spirit. With compassion for all parts of myself, I made room for whatever arose; it's okay if I want to hide from my grief at this moment, it's okay if I need to weep and stay in bed, it's okay if I want to clean and tidy up immaculately, it's okay if I want to revel in fleeting moments of ordinary pleasure without guilt. It's also okay if I'm simply feeling happy and being able to enjoy the present moment. It's okay if I'm angry, ashamed, guilty or relieved. I am okay this way or that. My grief may surprise me by surfacing in joyful times, but I allow it to linger as long as needed, embracing the entirety of this bittersweet farewell. And that is also okay, it is all OKAY.

Gradually, I nurture the wisdom that my healing takes place the moment I decide to surrender to that tightrope where the rational and spiritual meet – this is the sacred point where healing occurs. I reach out to this point as often as I need.

In fact, it has become a discipline in my everyday life where I give my body, mind, and soul to the sweet nectar of the Rational x Spiritual.

The arrival of truest Self – me unfiltered!

I found that I had become my mum's alter ego as I was growing up. My thoughts, behaviours and my actions were a mini, more modernised version of hers. This realisation hit me only after I lost her.

And I decided I don't want to be my mom. Not because I didn't like who she was, only because I realised I didn't know who I was. I was a living robot to her voice and instructions in my head even after she passed.

We grow up in the shadow of our parents, living within the beliefs and moral boundaries that our parents draw for us, and we forget to teach our children to find their own voice. I found my voice only after I lost my mom. Today, it's how I feel both, the excruciating pain of losing my mom and the sweet power of finding myself. I learnt that I never want to fit into a mould that is sculpted by someone else... neither do I want to sculpt a mould for my children. I am their guiding voice, not their primary voice. There is so much power in learning to live in one's own skin, aware of who one is and who one wants to be. No shame, no guilt, and a complete unconditional acceptance of who one truly is.

And it took me the loss of my mom to grow up… to learn to parent myself, be there for myself and love and accept all three: the child, the parent, and the adult versions of me.

Finding my power – a bittersweet experience

I still miss her. While there is freedom in self-discovery, some days, the burden of this autonomy makes me ache for the safe sanctuary of my mum's unconditional embrace.

This painful win of my autonomy seems like a crushing weight without her reassuring touch to help me carry it.

But I would never resign this strength arising from loss. This heartfelt profound intimacy with myself is my truest guide. It leads my way clearer than any external light ever could. It has helped me develop a healthier intrapersonal relationship, healthier interpersonal relationships, and become a better parent to my children.

The paradox here is that the more powerful I feel, the easier I find it to be vulnerable and this just makes life so much easier.

Today, it is my own burden I carry and loading or unloading the pain that is still with me is my choice because it is purely mine.

Self-awareness and self-acceptance have strongly anchored me.

Inner strength and spiritual surrender

Every time I think about my mom's passing, I am reminded about the futility of life. It reminds me that my time is limited and I cannot control this, but what I can control is what I do with the time I have.

Control is an illusion. When we surrender this blurry

illusion of control, we can clearly see direction. My surrender entailed a discovery of my core values, priorities, negotiables, non-negotiables, micro and macro visions for my precious life, and the importance of happiness. Facing life's impermanence head-on definitely made me infinitely present.

My personal growth has made me less afraid of my grief and my sadness.

I allow myself to miss my mom today. I provide my inner child the space to mourn and the inner adult the comfort. And when nothing works, I also allow myself to go into silence and process whatever emotions need to be. Tending to the gentle flow of our emotions holds the key to infinite growth and progress.

Helping someone ride the stormy waves of grief

When daily functioning is disrupted by pain and suffering, seeking support becomes critical. Trusted confidants, grief-support communities, spiritual groups or mental-health professionals can facilitate emotional health and healing. Left unchecked, sorrow can erode jobs, relationships and overall wellbeing through isolation, lethargy, despair and even ideas of self-harm. Processing grief in healthy ways not only helps us heal but prevents suffering from spreading into our environment.

If someone close to you is grieving loss, support involves offering immeasurable comfort.

• Be present: Initiate contact and make space for the person to cry, hug, scream, laugh, talk or even be silent. Facilitate raw catharsis.

• Show up consistently: Emotionally-loaded days like birthdays or anniversaries can be very difficult when we lose our loved ones to the unknown.

• Listen with compassion: Sometimes patience and non-judgemental presence outweighs advice. Simply showing up and sharing energy may lighten their load.

• Divert their mind: Enjoy fresh air together, watch a funny movie, eat comfort food – anything evoking lighter-hearted moments.

• Practical support: Relieving daily burdens by helping with chores, meals, or childcare reduces the mental, emotional and physical load.

• Move on: NEVER ever urge them to "move on". Healing involves gradually learning to move forward and live without our bereaved ones but not necessarily forget them. Grief never really ends; the loss integrates into meaning while sustaining an eternal soul connection. Their unique grief timeline must be respected while they strive to develop a healthy relationship with grief.

As I write this, grief has come up again while I recall the bittersweet memories of my darling mother. I process these feelings and memories, I feel the pain, but also understand that I am healing beautifully. Healing doesn't mean being devoid of emotions and erasing memories. Healing is being able to be inclusive of everything that was, is and will be. This reminds me of my capacity to surrender as there is no destination when it comes to grief. It simply is.

I discovered my capacity to surrender as I watched my

mother give in to the forces that demanded her passing. She didn't lose control; she gained control as she chose not to fight. She chose to get liberated as she peacefully surrendered to the process of her own death, breath by breath she gently flowed into transition.

She simply let go and let God.

Diving into the self

1. When encountering a profound loss, do you find yourself embracing and working through your emotions, or do you tend to avoid or suppress them?

2. What are the potential benefits to creating a safe space for yourself to face and work on your grief?

3. Can you describe in detail what your personal sanctuary looks like – a place or practice where you feel safe to process your emotions?

4. During times of loss and sorrow, how do you differentiate between aspects of the situation that you can control and those that you cannot?

5. What strategies can you use to practise accepting and letting go of the aspects of the situation beyond your control?

6. In what ways can acknowledging and accepting the unchangeable aspects of your situation, while respecting your emotional journey, contribute to your strength and healing?

7. How does self-compassion support your healing process, and how can you actively cultivate it?

8. How can engaging in creative or expressive activities help you process and understand your emotions during a

time of loss?

9. What are some mindfulness or meditation practices that might help you navigate your emotions and find inner peace during difficult times?

10. What are some effective ways to provide authentic support and compassion to someone who is grieving?

Blooming Florets

My Voyage into Parenting

I got pregnant with my daughter when I was 26 years old. It was an unplanned pregnancy, which I discovered when I was already seven weeks along.

Lying in my doctor's clinic, I was awestruck by a petite fluttering bean on the screen – my baby's heartbeat singing out like a rhythmic primordial tune. My baby girl, who is tall and all grown up now, was once so small and fragile like a bean. That transcendent captivating sound still echoes through my being.

My pregnancy was strenuous and demanding. I was barely able to hold down food or drink for five distressing months. I was tired and fearful and struggled with the thought of keeping my little bean safe. At six months, I was panic-stricken due to bleeding alarmingly. I was ordered a full bedrest until I stabilised. Throughout my pregnancy, I fought with feelings of loneliness. I felt like it was just my bean and I. My increased discomfort led to feelings of anxiety. I doubted my ability to safely receive and deliver my most precious gift ever. Only after my baby grew large enough for me to feel her communication did I start feeling rested. Her spirited twisting, turning and kicking in my womb gave me supreme joy. I could battle my fear with ease and surrender to the journey of blossoming into motherhood.

Hearing the melodious song of her first cry and embracing Sahana's newborn body resting on my heart washed away all the reminiscent fear in an instant. She miraculously healed nine arduous months through the glorious blessing of her tiny yet magnificent perfection.

I was overwhelmed by my new role. It was the most important role I may have ever played. I had to keep her healthy, alive and make her a whole adult. I distrusted others with my fragile newborn but felt desperately alone when choosing to stand guard solo. My postpartum depression intensely took over – fatigue, anxiety, sadness, frustration sitting on a pendulum between sleeplessness and hormonal changes.

My postpartum depression was heavy and my C-section stitches took extremely long to heal. Post-partum depression occurs due to hormonal changes in the body post-delivery along with changes that occur due to reduced sleep and overworking, and sometimes even lack of support at home.

I eventually decided to seek help and get it treated and it is only then that I started feeling better. A few simple ways to treat post-partum depression are:

• Counselling – to process feelings through this transitional life phase with an empathetic professional

• Practical help such as childcare, meals, household duties – to allow yourself time to rest, eat nutritiously, and rediscover simple self-care rituals

• Connect – keeping in touch with friends or new-mother support groups to ease isolation

• Outdoors – taking daily walks for mood-lifting fresh air, movement, and change of scenery every day

• Breathwork or meditation – practice to relax the nervous system and cultivate mental peace (this worked wonderfully for me)

• Extra support – consulting a psychiatrist regarding medication if symptoms feel unmanageable

• Narrative – reminding yourself often that this intense period of adjustment is temporary and that you will regain your joy and vibrancy

My little bean – resilient and reborn

My daughter was training to be a professional swimmer, and her dream was to become a national champion. She made it to the pool every single day, swam in the lanes, and worked extremely hard to make her dream come true for a good three years. She loved the water and loved her workout in the water even more. She then followed up her swim with a land workout to strengthen her muscles. Though she loved her training, there was something terribly amiss. Both her coaches and I found her general body alignment amiss and watched her struggle to do her activities in a straight line. We pushed her hard, but she pushed herself even more. She was determined to make her dream come true. She was driven and passionate. She even made it at 6 a.m. on cold rainy mornings to learn from her seniors.

Then Covid hit and life came to a halt.

When Covid halted life's rhythms, the basics of life – hobbies, school, and socialising – were all dictated by the screen. Entire worlds connected through screens as we trapped into lockdowns after lockdowns for unknown periods of time. A few isolated months into Covid, I noticed an imbalance in my daughter's back. One of her shoulder blades was protruding out while the other rested perfectly against her spine. Alarmed yet hesitant to face what was waiting for my confrontation, I decided to procrastinate. I convinced myself the asymmetry was harmless, fearing the realities I felt unready to confront.

But life does not spare anyone. The trials for the unprepared often hit hard.

As I rested comfortably in oblivion hiding from reality, my daughter suffered an acute lower back spasm. I hurried her into physical therapy to discover that there really was a deeper issue. My daughter's spine was severely curved and she had a condition called scoliosis. It is a condition in which the spine develops a deformity due to a sideways curve, resulting in asymmetry and rotation of the vertebrae.

After meeting the spinal surgeon, we learnt that surgery might be inevitable but could be postponed for years with intensive therapy.

Suddenly my nine-year-old bean's life path took a harsh turn. Her days became all about therapy – land therapy, aqua therapy, and then, counselling and talk therapy to process her turmoil. Her condition worsened and she was forced to endure bullying over her visible deformity. Her condition made her give up championship dreams and extinguished her hope and ambitions.

For four years, we helplessly watched her suffer, desperate to protect our delicate baby from the devastating fate that awaited her. The truth of her unavoidable surgery stiffened us with every passing day. We submitted her to examination after examination, shrinking away from the finality of each verdict. We managed to cling to fleeting hope that somehow her spine would miraculously realign.

Her stoic and strong father, or at least he prefers to project it that way, sat with daunting silence and pale white skin impatiently waiting for the final report to emerge. And there it came, the harshness of her reality hit us like boulders made of steel. There would be no eluding the surgeon's table for our precious baby girl. Possessed by dread, her strong father cried helplessly.

In that moment of turmoil and fear, I was clouded with disbelief. My mind refused to believe what my eyes were seeing and what my ears were hearing. I could summon no words or wisdom to soften the sharp edges of the despair that was cutting through us both. My mind had come to an eerie halt.

My once-unburdened, fragile little bean quickly shape-shifted into a warrior princess. She was the only one who could truly help herself. She confronted depression, persevered through gruelling regimens and took recourse to all the support needed. She was determined to reclaim agency over her body when few could relate to her challenge. Finally, one month before turning 13, she begged us and her doctor for surgery. She was done being worn down by constant pain and isolation. I remember my little wise one's words, "I can see my future, ma, I want to claim it and free myself of this burden on my back." With broken hearts yet bursting with hope and pride, her father and I went ahead and booked the date of her rebirth with the doctor.

I so vividly remember those eight agonising hours when my daughter went under the knife. Every minute passed achingly until she emerged out of the operation theatre three inches taller. Her blinding optimism despite brutal pain left everyone awestruck. The elated nurses urged the doctor to dismiss this super-girl by day four as she defiantly limped the halls, resolute in her resolve to go home. And so, she did. She made it to her own bed on day five using the power of her magical mind, restored and ready to reclaim life – my undefeatable warrior princess.

Showers of grace

With God's grace, my daughter's surgery was a success, her strong body was healing steadily. But I found sadness swirling within her, my confusion needed me to unveil its source – she was grieving her former life. Her old body bearing a deformity on her back, twisted shoulders and jeers from peers. Though she happily embraced her restored symmetry, and she welcomed the girl her experiences were moulding her into, but she also mourned the girl she lost along the way. She expressed the awareness that she needed some time to grieve her own loss to be able to dive unabashed into her newfound freedom. My little bean had grown up overnight. My heart welled up as she asked me for the space to allow her to go through the complete process of healing, stage by stage. I left my battered yet resilient baby within the cocoon of her creating to claim agency not just over her body, but also her destiny.

My little bean had explained in her sweet childlike words that she needed space to fully honour both versions of herself, her past and her present – validating the wisdom she had gained through unrelenting adversity. Those words of wisdom, although delivered through a child's vocabulary, braced my mind, body and soul with the essence of timeless truth. She had understood what took me decades to learn – that progress and sacrifice go hand in hand, that death and rebirth are day and night, and that no journey makes it into light without first going through the passage of darkness.

Pain and pleasure can co-exist. One doesn't need to be eradicated for the other to survive. Maybe one thrives because of the other. The beauty, elegance and faith with which she – my little bean, my little warrior princess – taught me this golden life lesson has left such a painfully beautiful mark in my soul.

The rented womb gifted my son

Sahana's father and I both cherished close bonds with our siblings and we were certain our daughter deserved the same. She consistently requested a playmate from the moment she could speak. We agreed that our family needed one more member and began trying to conceive again.

But I ended month after month in disappointment and tears, then eventually devastation. We decided to have an assisted pregnancy through IVF. Exploring this brought no success either.

I spiralled into obsession, taking each failure as a personal indictment. I blamed myself for being defective. Only after my tests confirmed ovarian health did I redirect blame toward her father. But his health checked out as well and now who is to blame? God!

After six invasive IVF attempts, my OB-GYN intervened. He refused further procedures citing medical risk. Finally, he suggested surrogacy using my remaining viable embryos. With hope wrapped in caution and realistic optimism, we proceeded and miraculously conceived on the first transfer.

Our roles as parents corroded the loving bond their father and I once shared. Our foundation began eroding painfully. My tunnel-visioned obsession with being a perfect parent to one and getting pregnant with the other sparked friction; we turned our united dream into a battleground. I suddenly found that we had left no space to voice fears or seek reassurance. I look back to discover that maybe expressing vulnerability might have saved us both.

Rather than pausing to nurture our shaken connection and strengthen our foundation amid relentless setbacks, we hurtled forward. We neglected the primary pillars of this unit – each other. In the blinded quest to mould the "perfect" nuclear family, we forfeited micro moments of joy that might have held us together. Our date nights died a slow death and our affection towards each other withered as we slipped into tailored "roles". The technicalities displaced romance, intimacy and companionship.

Parenting and assisted reproduction can profoundly strain relationships. But they need not break. Partners who consciously nurture empathy, gently communicate and prioritise each other's emotional wellbeing can surpass the challenges that come with these new roles of adulting. This is a shared journey. Tender love and care will provide all the support that is needed to be received by and returned to each other.

Though we emerged scarred, today the father of my children stands as my closest confidant, an unwavering father and my dearest friend. We lost the romance and intimate companionship along the way but with patience and compassion, even the most disconnected relationships can be gently realigned. They may mould into a new form and, yet, flow stronger. It is the conditioning of the "shoulds" and "should nots" that can deeply damage a relationship and blur clarity. Greater clarity of priorities, self-love and compassion towards each other can illuminate a hopeful path forward together, however defined!

Our budding family – our way

I have never really been one to make decisions based on others' opinions nor has he. As self-assured adults, we don't care much about complying with societal pressures and worrying about what other people have to say. "*Log kya kehenge* (what will people say?)" is not something that has ever bothered us. We went ahead and consciously chose surrogacy to expand our family, and we swiftly committed to being transparent and honest about our way forward.

It was a deliberate decision to reject secrecy and build an honest foundation for our family.

Our logic was clear – we refused to burden our family with the weight of secrets. Hiding foundational truths can create massive long-term emotional and physical turmoil. The arrival of our baby was bringing with it bright, beautiful and magical happiness. We refused to adulterate our blessing under the dark shadows of lies. Over time, it can gravely hurt relationships and mental health.

We refused to meet our baby with dishonesty, no matter what the judgements it invited. From the moment he was born, we pledged that he would only know unconditional love and belonging. He would learn at a young age that truth is liberating and rests on steady unshakeable pillars.

My doctor told me that over 10 women in my area were wearing tailored wombs and maternity clothes to hide a surrogate pregnancy. I was struck deeply by this and we decided to model forthrightness and be exemplary in our community. No one can hurt us by judgement if we are unapologetic, open and unabashed about our own reality.

The truth is, no one directly confronted us or our loved ones about our decision nor did anyone question our need for transparency. We don't know what was said behind closed doors, but we do know that we are proud of our personal choices and we live with the freedom of having nothing to conceal. Our son at the age of eight not only knows but also understands the circumstances of his conception. He celebrates his unique entry into this world with pride, he feels unconditionally loved and cared by a family overflowing with devotion for him and his sister.

Surrogacy – a topsy-turvy rollercoaster ride

The most intimidating challenge I faced was daunting fear and insecurity – acute anxiety over surrendering my baby's gestation to another woman's body. I lost the seed stage that the beautiful journey of motherhood entailed – the carrier. I grieved as my baby made it through milestones through the pregnancy. I pined for the feeling of his first fluttering kicks, the gentle swell of him growing within me, the twists and turns. I missed the nausea, the weight, the sleepless nights even. It all seemed like such a small price to pay for the security that came with holding my own baby. My anticipation grew into enduring helplessness. The wait was endless. The excitement of his arrival led to exhilarating ups full of hope and joy, while the downs were painful, fearful and extremely insecure.

In hindsight, I can confidently say that the nine months of surrogacy were the hardest time emotionally. I chose not to live in the now, I did not surrender to faith and created more pain by worrying over things I couldn't control. I chose to refuse support and avoided dealing with my painful feelings when I most needed to process and release.

Fear holds on to a false illusion of control. We try to hold on tight to this inexistence and drive ourselves into a pool of anxiety, worry and unhealthy thoughts. Surrendering this illusion of control helps us harness tools to mindfully cruise through stress. The woman I have become today understands the importance of emotional, mental, physical and spiritual self-care while navigating through complex waters. I now understand that I might have spared myself so much torment and emerged stronger if I had learnt to surrender and be at peace with unexpected outcomes sooner in life.

The arrival of our baby

All my challenges faded away the moment I held my son as I bathed him in my tears of love, joy, and relief. My baby... my little lion cub had made it to me. He fought through all the odds and made it into his mother's arms. His delivery was a planned C-section. So, his father, his sister and I planned a long trip to the USA to divert our minds from the anxiety of waiting for our baby. We were in New York, and I woke up one morning to find a mail from the surrogacy centre informing me that the surrogate had been admitted and was ready to deliver the baby anytime soon. Here we were, my little baby's core family sitting seven seas away in a whole other country, and this baby was ready to impatiently pop into the world way before time. Panic took over, and his father and I tried everything in our capacity to jump into the first available flight but to no avail; all the flights were full. We got in touch with the centre, and they said they would try to hold on till we were back. Five days later, we were back home, and two days later, our little one made a grand entry. As the three of us stood outside the operation theatre waiting impatiently for the arrival of our little princess (we were convinced it was a girl except for my daughter – she just knew she was having a little brother), we heard loud, husky crying. The doctor handed over our little baby to me... our little son. He was pale white with light eyes and the pinkest lips. I held him close to my chest and stuck his cheek to mine; he smelled so divine and so familiar. It took me back to the day my daughter was born – when I experienced the truest form of love for the first time that day. I felt like I had no idea what love was until I held my little baby girl and heard her cry right in my ears. The same feelings of love encased my entire being. The same feelings took over me while I held my son. He was mine, and I was so blessed in that very moment. After nine months of waiting, it took his arrival to bring me to the present moment.

There has been no looking back since then.

I recall a singularly profound moment; it was life-changing for me. As the doctor whisked my newborn son away for clean-up and further examination, I waited impatiently for my baby to make it back into my external womb – my arms. I was deluged by a wave of complex emotions – both grief and gratitude intertwined. Months ago, I had mourned the loss of being the gestational carrier of my baby; now the gestational carrier is going to mourn the loss of being a mother to the baby she harboured. I owe everything to the surrogate, the

Goddess who had tenderly nurtured him from a seed to a full-grown human for me to hold him at last.

At the time, we were prohibited in India from contact with the surrogate. This selfless woman gifted me the honour of motherhood through sacrifice. I pleaded with the doctor to let me see her, the Goddess who had suffered through labour's agony to deliver my greatest blessing. Looking at my face laced with a mix of intense emotions, I don't think he could get himself to say no.

I went in to the recovery room and sat at her feet and watched her sleep for some time. This stranger now felt like sacred family. She gave wholly of herself so I could finally cradle my son and mother him into the man he is meant to be. I stroked her forehead and eventually touched her feet and gave her the honour that a true Goddess deserves. I blessed her from the depths of my heart and left the observation room before she woke up.

This feeling of gratitude changed my life because I started learning from then the most profound lesson of unconditional gratitude. I am remembering how profoundly one compassionate being altered the landscape of my heart and made the divine practice of gratitude a daily habit.

The father – silent, gentle yet strong

Alongside mothers, fathers are pivotal contributors and fulfil an irreplaceable role nourishing children's emotional wellbeing. Beyond rule enforcement and material provisions, kids seek security, physical and emotional comfort from dads' strong yet gentle presence. A father's active, empathetic involvement can build self-confidence and resilience, promote inner growth and overall wellness. It profoundly influences social, cognitive, and physical development trajectories.

The father-child bond shapes relational models just as much as the mother-child bond. A nurturing relationship teaches kids what secure, healthy attachments feel like. A gentle empathetic dad is exemplary of partnerships his daughter might naturally seek for herself. She might instinctively attract relationships that support her self-worth and provide emotional availability. Sons on the other hand emulate fathers to a large extent. They draw self-confidence from their fathers by seeking approval along with gentle yet assertive course correction.

A father's purpose extends far beyond the traditional prototype of simply catering to breadwinning duties. He is a vital emotional anchor alongside mom. A father is equally capable of sensitive caretaking when stereotypes are cast aside and emotions are nurtured. Kids thrive best when holistically nourished by a harmonising parenting tapestry created by both parents.

The love that our children evoke comes straight from the soul. It is intense, limitless and all-consuming. Parental love can be deeply pure yet topped with fear. As parents, we realise nothing is more precious than our kids, not even ourselves. I find myself struggling in a battle with myself. I want to encourage my kid's independence and I want them to soar high and touch the sky. But I also fight the urge to clip their wings and give into my own need to protect and cocoon them. We constantly struggle between encouraging their independence and restricting their freedom to manage our anxiety. This boundless devotion paired with overprotection creates relentless conflict and guilt as we question our decisions.

Our children rapidly mature, oblivious to the fact that their growth continually impacts our fragile inner selves. We are confronted with difficult emotions head-on as they reach each new milestone. All I have to give my children is unconditional, judgement-free support overflowing with love and kindness. My heart knows no other way to love them.

I wonder who is growing at lightning speed?

Them or us?

Our children may outgrow our shoes, but as parents our hearts grow infinitely large – it's beyond our imagination.

Diving within the self

1. What are the essential emotional needs of your children to feel fully supported and loved?

2. How do you and your children foster and sustain a deep, mutual connection?

3. How can you effectively manage the emotional complexities that arise from your child's health as they grow?

4. What strategies can you use to create and uphold a positive and nurturing environment for your child?

5. How can you prioritise your mental and emotional health throughout your parenting journey?

6. What practices can help you cultivate and sustain unconditional love for your children, especially during their

challenging transitional periods?

7. How can you approach disciplining your children with a balance of gentle understanding and assertiveness?

8. In what ways can you provide unwavering and unconditional support to your children as they navigate their personal challenges?

9. What actions can you take to ensure that your love and support for your family remain strong through open communication and trust even in difficult times?

10. How can you balance being a parent with other roles and responsibilities in your life?

My Worth

My Glory

My entire life, my self-worth has been based on my relationship with money. My self-esteem has been an emotional battle and has always been connected to my ability to make free financial choices. I started earning tremendously well at the age of 17 and I become financially independent.

But I spent that money recklessly, taking my financial freedom for granted since I felt I could always fall back on patriarchal social structures for support if needed. I've somehow always found so much comfort in the patriarchy that I deeply believed in it. My self-worth was based on superficial exteriors – it was also based on my appearance, not how beautiful I truly felt inside but how others made me feel. I spent huge amounts of money on expensive clothes and things, to prove to people that I am worth and to gain the validation that I was of value. Overall, my relationship with money, people and my environment was toxic. But what I really suffered from was a toxic relationship with myself. I was choosing to poison myself with thoughts, beliefs and behaviours that I didn't need to survive or thrive.

I had it all – male attention, a successful modelling career, money, friends, creative outlets like art and writing, freedom and skill. Was I good enough then? Not enough. So then, I gave it all up to find my self-worth and get validated through familial roles – perfect partner, doting mother, good daughter, cultured daughter in-law. I still felt a profound sense of not being good enough in the depths of my being.

This nagging feeling of "not enough" led me to endlessly seek more – more love, more validation, more shopping, more praise. The void was like a bottomless pit. I bent over backwards compromising 'myself', 'my true self', 'my self-worth'. I altered my thoughts, needs, desires, and beliefs to gain external acceptance. But even when I achieved some external validation, it wasn't enough. I was never enough and the emptiness remained. I was never able to accept, value or love myself fully for who I was. My relationship with my own inner being was broken at my core. I was never enough for ME.

Finding my worth – breaking through the patriarchy

I believe that in a male-dominated society, my sense of self-worth was dependent on the acceptance or rejection

I received from the man. I felt constantly spun around, oscillating between the opinions of the man's whims. Financial empowerment became my ticket to independence. Money gave me the freedom to be, to pursue my dreams and desires, and even to love from a more empowered position. Unfortunately, most men may respect an empowered woman yet simultaneously fear and try to clip her wings.

But it's easy to blame society or men. I chose to play the blame game but every choice I made was mine alone. Every decision I took was my choice. And every accusation I hurled was also my choice. Blaming external forces was simpler than taking responsibility for my own actions and choices. But it only left me powerless.

Owning my choices and taking responsibility for my life makes me powerful. I very willingly chose to give away my power to everyone around me, chasing the illusion of validation.

I have long feared embodying the "abla nari" archetype of the helpless woman. Encountering the helpless woman would trigger me intensely. Even through my work as a psychologist, I either wanted to rescue them or shake them up. I would get so emotional about helping them find their power that I may have landed up disempowering them further. I would wonder why they affected me so deeply. I realised they reminded me of the vulnerable little girl I had locked away inside, despised, and rejected. I tried hard to embrace her at times but the closer I came to my helpless inner child, the feelings of worthlessness would stare me in the face. Embracing my womanhood has always been terribly challenging, it was so much easier to embrace the patriarchy instead. My toxic relationship with myself reflected in the world around me. Yet I chose to daily drink the poison of self-sabotage, blaming others rather than taking responsibility. I was sickened by the fragile feminine part of me that knew my deep, dark wounds and repelled her by locking her away. I created unsurmountable boulders that clouded my self-worth and deeply struggled to embrace myself as a woman.

Victim or victor?

I found it easier to tie my sense of self-worth to money – so rational, unemotional, no triggers and no messy vulnerability. I had the whole world to blame rather than take responsibility. But I still felt sick and unhappy inside of me. I was the biggest victim I knew, everything felt meaningless yet I was strangely deserving and entitled. The ultimate victim, yet expecting rescue – not empowered at all. Why should anyone else save me? We each have a responsibility for our own lives and choice is a power we hold. I was quick to blame patriarchy yet I supported the system through my own beliefs and actions. Choosing victimhood is giving away power and taking responsibility is reclaiming power.

So now I smugly ask myself – who is to truly blame for my situation?

Me. And, as I answer, I find my POWER.

My power

Today, I embrace the woman I'm becoming. I aspire to be independent and powerful, while I still find myself cherishing my capacity for vulnerability and interdependence. I consciously make choices that align with my own sense of self – seeking comfort from within and not validation from others. Accolades may come – I still love to nurture my external beauty as much as I enjoy my relationship with money – but my worth is not defined by glory, it is undefined. What matters most is acceptance of the woman I am – my femininity, my strength, the abla nari, the masculine energy within me, the darkness, the light and everything I am. My identity is still unfolding; I am still discovering but the search for some perfect "me" will no longer determine my self-worth. Rejecting any part of me reduces all of me. I hold myself tight, wrapped within my own cocoon of unconditional love, acceptance and safety. I will not diminish myself and I will never dim my own light again no matter what arises within me or around me.

I shall not allow myself to be defined. I am fluid and evolving.

Working with my inner child

To move past our traumas and old wounds into self-assured and self-loving individuals, we must address the wounded inner child still clinging to those painful memories and fears. As adults now, we have grown from that moment and have the power of choice. This connects back to our innate superpower – the power of perspective. We always have the ability to view all sides and consciously choose our point of view, self-concept, and eventually, our actions.

First, we need to embrace the victim within, the part stuck

in survival mode, with love, empathy and zero judgement. Choosing victimhood is unhealthy but understandable, because we may know no better; we are only trying to cope and survive. Our inner child may not always have the understanding of clarity and choice. Anger, resentment, hatred, or guilt towards our inner victim and ourselves are equally unhealthy and harmful defences.

Our frightened inner child requires empathy and patience to safely release the pain, accept that they endured what they may not have understood, and recognise that now the inner adult has the agency to let go, heal and make new choices. We alone have the power to determine ourselves.

Core characteristics of the victim

• Helplessness: Victims are that child within us who cannot see the way forward and feel helpless.

• Complaining: Blaming and complaining are unhealthy ways to cope with helplessness and regain some sense of power.

• Self-confirmation bias: Assuming that others are constantly angry at or disappointed in them justifies retreating further into the zone of victimhood and shutting others out.

• Mind-reading: They expect people to read their mind and rescue them without having to communicate directly. Expressing vulnerability feels threatening.

• Overthinking: It is underacting in disguise. It creates an illusion of action and responsibility. In reality, it fosters paralysis and is a core ingredient in the zone of victimhood.

• Fundamentally unsafe: This type of feeling is rooted in

irrational core beliefs that come from unhealed trauma from the past. This trauma usually resides within the inner child and children can easily feel fearful and helpless.

• Victim narrative: This is the self-concept around past victimisation with statements like, "You know what happened to me..."

• Self-sabotage: Knee-jerk self-sabotage reactions in difficult situations are a self-fulfilling prophecy that the world is against them, stopping forward movement or taking responsibility.

• Childlike emotional responses: Reverting back to immature, childlike emotional responses clouds rational thinking when stressed.

• Clinging to the past: This means dwelling on past offenses, bringing them up in new fights rather than seeking resolution. It even manifests as retelling stories of wounds to strangers to get them emotionally invested and then using guilt about abandonment.

• Exhaustion: Victims are often exhausted. They have to repress how they really think and feel. They have to repress their strengths and talents or people might stop feeling sorry for them.

• Physical illness: This is more so due to the mental exhaustion, which further makes people feel sorry for them.

To summarise, the victim mentality leverages unhealthy coping mechanisms like the ones mentioned above to bring balance to the distressed anxious state. There is a lack of personal responsibility, agency and growth. The victim feels disempowered, stuck and oppressed, unaware of the fact that it is self-imposed.

Coming to terms with and accepting that one may be stuck in the victim zone is a courageous and liberating step to take for oneself. It is nothing to be ashamed of, but in fact a positive step towards healing and reaching one's highest, most authentic self. It is as simple as unlearning something we learnt when we didn't know better – no judgement, no bias, simply unlearning.

Beating the victim

Shedding victimhood can feel threatening – like unpeeling a part of ourselves and laying it to rest. Fear, grief and even insecurity may arise as we release old coping strategies that once anchored us. Our inner victim stood by us when we felt alone and lacked better tools. Compassion and empathy for the fact that we coped and survived with each step is the cornerstone for ease and release. A therapist or trusted friend can help us through this transition.

But…

Sometimes we truly are victims and that's also okay. Sometimes situations are truly beyond our control, we are genuinely scared, something did really break our morale and so on. And that's okay. But the problem occurs when we get stuck in this hook of victimhood. Breaking out of victimhood requires internal work. We need to learn to take back our power where we do have control. By lovingly hand-holding our frightened inner child with external support, we can manage to move on and take our power back.

Some tips on how to take the power back:

Prayer and Faith

For me, my biggest go-to is prayer and faith. It somehow has the power to clear my mind and help me then see the rational and work in a mature fearless manner. Meditation helps me clear my mental space and reach out to my superpower of perspective. The spiritual grounding gives me the courage to come from an open-hearted space. Hope and responsibility become my standing ground over resentment, loneliness and despair.

Forgiveness

Resentment is poisonous; it is a poison that erodes only "us". This poison is only going to make us sick, make us suffer, damage our relationships, and kill our happiness, joy, success, and overall growth. Forgiving both ourselves and others is a powerful and integral part of the process. And this mostly comes from grace. Grace comes from prayer and faith.

Mood

Our moods are deeply swayed by the currents of the psycho-soma. Psycho being the mind and soma being the body. A peaceful mind gives rise to peaceful actions and a rested body gives rise to a clearer mind. Regulating emotions through mindfulness, exercise, creative flow, social connection, ample rest, and productivity fosters clarity and steadiness. Generosity and service to others and society can also empower by highlighting our ability to uplift others. It helps us focus on a macro-perspective rather than fixate on blaming.

Some of the hormones that influence overall mood:

• Serotonin: The stabiliser – thrives on meditation, gratitude, sunlight, and movement

• Dopamine: The reward chemical – surges from self-care, tasty foods, completing tasks, and celebrating small wins

• Endorphins: The painkiller – rushes in during laughter, hugs, exercise, dark chocolate, favourite scents and essential oils

• Oxytocin: The love hormone – gets activated by affectionate touch, playing with babies and pets

Taking ownership overshadows the victim.

Redirecting the story – reframing the narrative

"I am the master of my destiny, I am the captain of my soul." This is my most favourite line from the famous poem *Invictus* by William Ernest.

A narrative is the internalised and evolving story of the self that is constructed by the person to make meaning and sense out of their own life based on past experiences – traumatic, healthy and unhealthy. This narrative drives our reactions, choices and feelings about the self, our relationships and our environment.

Victimhood arises from narratives like: "Bad things just happen to me no matter what. Others are to blame, not me. I can't change what happens so why try?"

But we can consciously reframe the narrative, as Ernest empowers us to do. For example: "I am the creator of my own story", "I have the power to choose how I respond to bad things", "The person I will be and the impact I have on others is my power alone", "Life is not compassionate towards victims and I have the power to choose the path of growth towards my highest best and happy self."

Choosing to take charge of our thoughts, behaviours and actions builds agency. This inner power opens infinite possibilities beyond our limitations that may be built on redundant conditioning and fear. Perspective is our superhero and remembering we are the captain of our own ship is our Bat-mobile. We are not helplessly trapped in the alien attacks of the fearful mind but flying through with golden hope and limitless potential. If we believe ourselves helpless, we stay trapped in the darkness but believing in the autonomy we have over our inner world steers us into the vast expanse of growth and healing.

Changing the narrative is important because we are choosing to focus on something else over victimhood and tapping into our superpower of perspective.

Diving into the self

1. Reflect on a moment in your life when you felt powerless or victimised. What was that experience like?

2. What childhood experiences or beliefs might have contributed to your feelings of victimhood?

3. What external factors or relationships might reinforce your feelings of victimhood currently, and how can you address them?

4. Do you currently struggle with feelings of low self-worth

or disempowerment? What contributes to these feelings?

5. Write a letter to your inner child, offering unconditional love and acceptance to heal the parts of yourself that feel undervalued and powerless.

6. In what areas of your life do you tend to adopt a victim mindset?

7. What steps can you take to regain a sense of agency and reclaim your personal power?

8. How can you identify and acknowledge these self-defeating thoughts and patterns?

9. How do these patterns and thoughts affect your self-esteem and sense of personal empowerment?

10. What strategies like mindfulness and seif-awareness can you use to transform a self-defeating narrative into an empowering one?

Changing our inner narrative is vital. It transforms our thoughts, empowers us to shift our focus from victimhood and embrace the superpower of perspective.

Designed Dreams

Actualise Your Own Blueprint

The first dream I ever had as a child was to be able to help people. I always had this innate urge to help and heal people. I was the inevitable "go-to person" amongst my friends, and I always managed to find solutions to help my loved ones even as a kid. But I was so caught up in my own plethora of fears and insecurities that I lost myself along the way, and with that went away my dream.

But my very conscious dream always was to be a queen. I always wanted a crown on my head, and I gave up my dream to be a "Miss India" despite intense persuasion from my manager and organisation. I was so scared that I needed to be on stage in front of a thousand people and that I would stutter my way to failure. I was consumed with the terror of public failure and overwhelmed with thoughts of humiliation. My decision to retreat from my decades-old fantasy of being crowned a queen rode on excuses that led me astray.

I refused to take accountability for giving up on my dreams. That would also mean taking accountability for giving up on myself and facing my demons. I blamed external barriers, people, situations and made excuses for my life choices. This weight stayed with me until one day I decided it was time to let it go. Once I unconditionally embraced the truth that the power of our choices belongs to us, forgiveness flowed. I released the resentment, was able to forgive myself, my relationships and my environment. I was able to be more compassionate towards my fearful former self. The relief and ease that forgiveness and compassion brought within me gave me the courage to reclaim my dreams and chase after them.

My realisation got me to stumble upon two pivotal truths – dreams do not come with an expiry date and potential never fully fades.

I began to author the first chapter on pursuing my dreams. I did my postgraduate diploma in integrative counselling psychology and then went ahead and did my Master's in counselling psychology followed by chasing my dream to be queen.

Today, at 40, my childhood dreams stand fulfilled. I hold pride in both, my counselling practice and my hard-won pageant victory.

Breaking through the shell

My childhood passed with me behind the scenes, deep

inside a shell. The shyness was agonising. I could barely control my speech, and my stammer would burst out of me like an overflowing dam. I was terrified of public speaking and deeply feared humiliation when put in the spotlight. I pulled away from opportunities and hid from my peers, denying myself my own needs and ambitions. This self-isolation most definitely brought home safety but starved me like anorexia and stole me of fulfilment.

I was done with the loneliness this safety provided me, and decided to take charge and crush this fear by going through it and facing it head on. The highest challenge was putting myself in the limelight as I was done being afraid. I was no longer going to let fear rule my life. That's when I decided to start modelling, to take risks, blossom, and grow.

I started modelling early in life at the age of 17, quickly falling in love with the ramp and the glory bestowed by each empowering strut down that magnificent stage. This was where I took rebirth – I emerged again, but this time self-empowered.

There was this one time when I tripped on the ramp during fashion week. A very funny picture of me was pasted on the front page of a leading newspaper. Everyone seemed to be talking about it and I felt so much shame that my eyes welled up and all my old fears came alive. But I had become that girl who loved me, including my flaws and all. As I looked up, I saw so much laughter on everyone's faces but it no longer devastated me. I also saw warmth on the faces of my loved ones. Poise thrives not in perfection but how we reframe our stumbles knowing their arrival is inevitable. Encouraged by my loved ones and my own hard-won self-compassion, I decided that bravery is a choice. I had the power to choose to stand gracefully rather than crumble on the floors of external validation.

I can choose to allow people to define me or not.

I chose then not to be defined.

I choose now not to be defined.

The silent voice of doubt

I have spent a large part of my life questioning myself and struggling with self-doubt. And when it comes to my dreams, my speech has been a big barrier. I don't stammer in a destructive manner anymore but my fear about stammering on some days can be destructive even now and I must push through those feelings of fear on a regular basis.

It takes me back to the time I was in college and we had to make a group presentation. I had requested my friends to allow me to present. I was tired of feeling like a failure. I thought the presentation was a good way to conquer my lifelong dread. I hoped that it would help me find my voice.

My friends understood that I needed to do this. They supported me and lovingly expressed how proud they were of me. I prepared for the presentation like there was no tomorrow and I knew my part like the back of my hand. I knew I could do it and this time I was going to do it.

I believed I was going to be a success.

The morning arrived. I stood tall in front of my grade and glanced at my classmates. Most of them had expressions of happiness and support. My professor gleamed with pride at my bold step and when I looked backstage, my friends stood with big smiles and their thumbs up. I picked up my paper and looked back up. Began to say good morning and I got stuck at G. I never got past G – "gggggggggggggg," I went on. I stopped and I tried again but the "ggggggg" seemed endless. My patient friends and empathetic professor gave me the space to take as much time I needed. They had hope and chose to believe in me. But I failed, miserably failed, and there I was: the biggest loser, giving up on myself and my dream.

The entire room emitted only empathy but I drowned myself in contempt – there I was, playing a role I was used to, the defeated spectacle.

I tucked my head down and went backstage, mute once again. Someone had to take over and do my part. I never went back on a stage, and lost all hope. Frustration, disappointment and anger became my friends. My loving friends, family and professor tried everything to help me but to no avail.

Every time I get ready to go on a public platform, this scene plays over and over in head gripping me with fear.

My crowning glory

For me, the most difficult time was on the day of my finale for Mrs India. I wanted that crown so bad and had worked for it so hard for months on end, day and night. And then there were these question-and-answer rounds in front of a huge audience that I had to face. My fear of stammering had taken over me and my desperation to win had taken over.

This lethal combination made me feel not only mentally

ill but physically ill. I had to get that crown and my mind was refusing to rest and let go. I had completely lost the present moment and was either consumed with the failures and defeats of the past or the possibility of failing in the near future. Though I looked polished on the outside – dressed in a stunning black gown with beautiful full hair and makeup – inside I felt unsteady and desperate. Externally I felt like a Goddess and internally like a broken wreck. I felt incapable of tempering my swirling angst.

Recognising that no self-talk could calm my inner turmoil now, I gave up the inner fight and allowed discomfort to flow through me. I gave up battling my thoughts and fears but instead allowed them to pass and do their thing. I disconnected from my feelings of physical ill health, my hurting tummy, nauseous insides, spinning head, racing heart and allowed it to just be.

I prayed to God and called out to my Guru, remembering that I had the biggest gift life had bestowed upon me – my faith and my spiritual path. I had the healthiest tool in my body itself and that was my breath. I allowed my mind to dance with the rhythm of my breath and naturally calm my fraught nervous system. This rhythmic flow of in-and-out reminded me that whatever happens, I will still be breathing. Meditatively observing each inhale energised me and each exhale diffused churning thoughts and emotions. I started connecting back to myself. With spiritual solace re-centring me, I emerged calmer despite the surrounding chaos. I had isolated myself backstage, taken recourse within myself and disconnected from the mayhem.

About two hours later when things settled within me, I snapped right into the present moment. That very moment the stage lights came on and the first performance began. I ran into my lineup, let out a scream of excitement and joy and started dancing. My fellow queens (every woman is a queen regardless of a crown) danced with me and we ended in a group hug, wishing each other luck. No stammer, no tripping on stage, no quivering lips, no desperation, no shame, no fear, and no doubt. Everything melted away – the only thing that was present was me, completely present with myself in this very joyous moment.

And victory emerged the moment I released; it was fear and desperation that paralysed me.

I stand crowned as Mrs India Earth 2023. Scars and all. I encourage you to write your story without any external permission. Ignore notions of what you "can" and "cannot" do, what you "should" and "should not" do. Sometimes our dreams hibernate, but they flicker patiently like lights waiting to shine on us.

Your season will dawn and your light will shine, your HIGHNESS.

My circle of believers, not naysayers

Pursuing my dreams with razor-sharp focus and commitment to my authentic self was a catalyst for change across all my relationships. It took away a whole load of relationships but deepened my bond with others who are in my inner circle today. I have always preferred quality over quantity, a small and strong circle when cultivating community. This season of intense self-examination and barrier-breaking stripped away many relationships in my life. Relationships that were not firmly rooted and naysayers were pushed to shore by the strong ripple effect of my ambition. At the end of it all, the ocean of my life has my strongest connections and the people who matter the most lounging in the waters.

Today I feel a sense of gratitude about the chaos that hit my life before I decided to complete my Master's and take part in Mrs India. The isolation and betrayal from my close friends and community broke me to a point of feelings of no resurrection. The loose talk amongst my friends and the fact that my mother was struggling with the last stages of the big C made me feel so much fatigue. I felt finished, my personal reserves fell barren and I was overcome with sorrow and dread. But, in this season, I saw the truth and felt the love my true friends had for me. Life had shown me a mirror and reflected my genuine core relationships whose hands I hold even today.

And then strength awakened, like a phoenix I arose from ash. I decided to take part in Mrs India. The fatigue I felt before was now taken over by raw strength. I was propelled towards the horizons of my dreams and there was no stopping me. I was on my way from being "cancelled to crowned".

When I won the crown, my triumph reflected glory but also clarity. I bathed in the glorious light of my win but with my truest companions for life – my honest well-wishers and the sweetest tribe. My preexisting friends neither behaved differently, nor treated me differently. I was always their queen and they, my queens. We had always honoured the royalty that exuberated from each of us.

My tiny tribe offers unspoken assurance of belonging and unity. Our connection rests on true love and our relationships flow simply because I belong to them and they, to me. No laurels or accomplishments define our connection – it's love, pure love.

Standing in my truth – fulfilled and gratified!

The fulfilment of my dreams and my openness about them have most definitely influenced people around me. I was honest about my surrogacy journey both to live by my truth and to encourage others to do so. And today, I have strangers expressing gratitude for my surrogacy transparency. They felt permitted to expand their families. My eight-year-old symbolises hope beyond norms. He silences the shame as he shines his light and spreads joy everywhere he goes.

I have people come up to me and openly ask me questions about how I deal with my fears when it comes to my speech and what gave me the courage to chase my dreams and fight my fears. Seeing my voice strengthen and my dreams come true, it rekindles forgotten ambitions in friends. My neighbour dusted off her neglected manuscript; another friend talks about how she broke her barriers towards dancing and started a Zumba class by dismissing her embarrassment over her age. Someone randomly walked up to me during an event and told me she's changing careers and has started studying nutrition; another friend pursued her passion for diving and travel.

I do go through my own periods of doubt. But it is these stories of rediscovered resilience that relinquish my doubt and lift me back up. My fears and doubts linger, but I now recognise that the ripples of my victory may stretch farther than I can trace.

And that heroism is simply showing up with a courageous, open heart, come what may.

And the impact of that can go beyond imagination and even rationale.

And that the greatest teachings come from the wildest dreams, because dreams never fade, they persistently knock.

My dreams never left me. I may have given up on them but they arose from my soul and could not be extinguished. I tried to bury my dreams. The ache of their longing was too painful. Achieving my aspirations seemed impossible, so I constructed rationalisations to terminate them. But dreams don't die with ease; they demand a revisit and shapeshift to mould into the present till they are fulfilled.

Some ambitions require years of nurturing before their birth. And their only pathway to delivery is the vessel they have chosen. When our dreams are ready to manifest, age, sex, background, religion, country, race, capability and so on set no limits on destiny. We need to be willing to surrender fear and self-doubt to be able to meet with our dream. Taking a focused and bold step and walking hand-in-hand with inspiration guarantees the soul that it is seen, heard and understood. And this, your highness, is a non-negotiable.

When I compare the girl who hid from her dreams to the woman who had the courage to chase her dreams, the biggest difference I find is HAPPINESS. Maybe not hundred percent success but happiness – profound, resilient and infinite.

Eyes on the prize

I am currently balancing the pursuit of my dreams with my responsibilities and obligations. Our dreams are evolving and never-ending and so are our responsibilities and obligations. There's never a junction for a purpose-driven person where they don't have to make a choice. I find myself making this choice every single day.

We are constantly presented with choices and, in my case, it was between my terminally ill mother, my Master's, my little children and sometimes even choosing myself and my mental health. Then there was a conflict between my grave grief, my children, my exams for my MA, my grieving father, my duties at home, and myself and my mental health.

Today it is between my duties as a psychologist, my responsibilities as Mrs India Earth, my children, my duties towards myself and my loved ones, and so on. There is no absolutist formula to balance life. Any form of an extremist approach tips the scale. The point is to keep the scale balanced and shift the weight.

One needs to make the choice with absolute awareness and clarity of mind. This clarity of mind comes when we do away with any form of obsession towards any aspect of our life. For me this clarity comes with my daily spiritual practice. I find that on days when I do my breathwork and meditation in a disciplined way, I'm calmer, my mind is clear, I make better decisions, and I'm both rested and productive.

My dreams – unbound and timeless

I've never tailored my ambitions to external timelines, societal expectations and stereotypes. Ambitions are not dictated by the right age or gender, though the unfortunate truth is that, in most cases, society's standards are particularly harsher on women than men. I eventually flourished, but it took my own inner voice to lead me to my achievements.

Wisdom now guides me steadily. I am able to move onwards devoid of restlessness, hunger and blinding ambition driving each step.

I am learning to relish life's flavours enroute yet still move with a steady acceleration towards my vision with a sense of calm. My ambitious yet unforced pace drives me with balance and strength.

Like flowers that bloom with tender love and care with robust roots holding them strong from beneath, our dreams too blossom when tenderly nurtured yet held solid and strong.

And I have only just begun to bloom.

Unlocking my power

The heart is not defined by age or abilities. Every pending dream or desire is the little version of oneself that went unattended. The heart dreams and the brain make us question whether it will work or not. The mind may sometimes convince us that we have exceeded the limits of our viable boundaries. This fear-driven grip of the mind can be dismantled by self-belief and methodically addressing all conceived obstacles. The heart has a beautiful capacity to persuade the brain to align with destiny.

The heart embraces infinite possibilities whereas the mind sees finite resources. But by offering the mind strategic plans and calculated risks, the brain can befriend the heart to facilitate the impossible. Dreams require sweat, faith and patience to penetrate through the fog of self-doubt and fear.

Setting ambitious targets supported by short-term timelines, procuring support, focus, consistency, commitment and self-compassion through ups and downs become the building blocks of belief.

Belief in oneself and discipline are the truest forms of self-love when working towards making one's dreams come true.

Find a way to believe that the impossible dream in your heart can come true.

The irony is that the minute you truly believe this in your deepest core, the world will shift to make this possible, unlocking your hidden power.

Evolving through every life phase

My dreams have not changed, but rather have evolved. I have developed a larger perspective – shifting from "What do I want?" to "How can I help more people?", "How can I expand my voice's reach?" and "How can I go after what I want?" This change in my mindset has given me the courage to be vulnerable and open about my brokenness. I have come to realise that flaws do not define one's capability or their right to dreams and ambitions.

I view my brokenness through the Japanese art of kintsugi. A broken item isn't discarded but in fact the pieces are put back together with glue and adorned with gold. The items held together with the loving approach of kintsugi are more breathtaking than the original.

Similarly, my wounds glitter – like gold.

Every time I failed and picked myself up, every time I cried and topped it with a smile so that I can feel stronger, every time I felt like life was coming to an end and struggled to find a ray of hope, every time I thought of harming myself or ending my life and put my faith in God, every time it felt like I was drowning but managed to keep my nose up in the air, every time I failed over and over again but didn't give up and eventually succeeded are all my streaks of gold.

The golden glint of my kintsugi scars grant me pride, confidence and humility serving as my credential.

Let defiance rule – let magic happen

Moving beyond society's whimsical expectations, the only standards that matter are our own, unadulterated by age or gender. As long as we remain respectful without causing harm, we deserve to live free from the tyrannical societal chains binding us. Now that the rights to freedom and authorship have been established, let's discuss our infinite dreams.

We can start by accepting our boldest ambitions without judgement: "I am in complete acceptance of who I am and what I desire", "I wholly welcome these desires as a part of me". Surrender is the only way to release the tight grasps of fearing what lies beyond our control. The mother of surrender is faith – it is the provider of breathtaking freedom while we take the liberating freefall into the lap of fulfilled dreams.

Control is rooted in fear, surrender is cultivated by faith.

My fear of losing my future, my freedom and my financial independence made me chase the crown so hard that I forgot all about enjoying the process that day. It is only when I surrendered my thoughts, set my might to believe all will be well by turning to my practice and came into the present moment that I enjoyed my performance. I was in a state of enjoyment and surrender rather than grasping and grappling. I could go with the flow, observe myself and thanks to that moment I got to know myself better.

So, I advise the young and old, regardless of gender – dream big, chase your dreams, progress relentlessly, but don't lose sight of the happiness that resides in the here and now, not in some distant victory day.

Pause frequently to admire the beauty unfolding all the way, let fate guide you beyond your wildest dreams, stay anchored in the present moment and sway along the rhythm of your breath as you reach for the stars.

And that is where MAGIC happens.

Diving within the self

1. What actions do you think you could take that will drive you closer to your dreams?

2. How can you blur out society's arduous expectations and focus inwards towards your personal goals and expectations?

3. Create a list of your most cherished dreams and aspirations. Do these dreams feel distant or unattainable? What are the fears and doubts that make you feel this way?

4. Do you believe it's possible to take control of your own destiny? Why or why not?

5. What concrete steps can you take to start turning your dreams into reality, even if you face mental hurdles?

6. List the people in your life who offer unconditional, unwavering support and encouragement. How can you nurture and strengthen these supportive relationships?

7. How can you build an inner circle that boosts your am-

bitions and eliminates self-doubt?

8. How can you tune out society's demanding expectations and focus on your personal goals and desires?

9. How can you celebrate small victories on your path to achieving your dreams to maintain motivation?

10. How can you balance the pursuit of your dreams with the practicalities of daily life?

Design your own dreams, the canvas is wholly yours. Within you lies the potential to unlock your hidden powers.

Floundering Alchemist

Transcending Anxiety and Fear

I was a successful model in my late teens and early 20s. I started working so young, I was exhausted from the hustle of juggling my career and my studies. A part of me was tired and I thought I would find my escape through marriage. I felt relieved when I gave up my thriving modelling career to be the "good wife". I comfortably conformed to my lifelong conditioning and societal expectations. Quitting my career felt like a breath of fresh air.

The good wife, the good daughter, the good daughter-in-law, and the good girl were all screaming from inside looking for validation from the external world. I was trying to fit into a mould shaped by society. I gave it all up hoping to be praised for my selfless decision but it went unnoticed. In trying to prove my selflessness and worth, I had handed my power away, created an unhealthy co-dependency and stripped away my sense of self.

Most definitely, it wasn't one of my brightest decisions in life.

For years on end, I was consumed by resentment, anger and regret. I blamed everyone, including myself, for framing myself into this oppressed form with my own hands. My choices were self-defeating and driven by fear – fear of failure, and even bigger, fear of my own success. I dimmed my light in order to not shine brighter than others. I was afraid to stand in my own power, because if I stood too strong, people would abandon me.

I was terrified of overpowering the man, I was even afraid of overpowering my closest and most loved ones because, "What if they left me and I landed up alone?"

I will speak more on loneliness in a chapter that follows.

After years of self-work and much introspection, I started connecting to myself. I began to develop unconditional self-acceptance and self-love, and finally, decided to release the burdens I had inflicted on myself. My inner power unlocked and I was able to make healthy choices that aligned with my wellbeing. I was able to take charge and own my inner power.

I realised that choosing myself didn't mean excluding others. Neither was choosing myself an act of selfishness. I no longer needed external validation. I claimed my worth, embraced my freedom and eventually found my purpose.

Stumbling upon my ikigai – my love for psychology

This newfound version of myself who was free and bursting with her reclaimed power now needed purpose. Discovering my purpose involved much soul-searching and passionate exploration through trial and error.

I decided to study and stumbled upon a counselling certificate course. There came that fulfilling feeling, I belonged. But I only managed to finish one module and couldn't complete the rest of the course. My daughter needed me and I lacked time to complete it.

When I regained time a few years later, I had forgotten about my love of psychology. I tried on many other hats – soft-skills trainer, preschool teacher and nutrition. Though rewarding, something was amiss; I never felt like I belonged. And when my heart called me back to psychology, I belonged again.

My journey towards purpose has been long and winding, marked by confusion yet deep fulfilment. I'm thankful for the divine guidance and courage to make choices that honoured my soul's whispers.

I restarted my journey and jumped right into studying psychology – obtaining a diploma in counselling psychology and later a distinguished Master's as a counselling psychologist. My path gaining more and more clarity along the way, I felt deep love. Though the path twisted unexpectedly, I found my way back – I had found my IKIGAI.

Now I can serve wholeheartedly with expertise. I'm grateful for the journey that prepared me. It gave me the courage to make choices for ME and to find my purpose. My purpose is not just WHAT I do but WHO I am. My heart fills up with emotion when I say that I am living proof of the fact that we can reclaim our power and follow our hearts to our home – where we belong.

This was also the time when anxiety had become my unwelcome companion. I was pursuing my purpose in psychology alongside supporting my ailing mother and daughter. I felt profoundly tested, exhausted and the light at the end of the tunnel seemed to have drastically dimmed. The caretaking needs, assignments, and exams exhausted my body, made my mind swirl with fear, shattered my heart and clouded all of me with cyclones of guilt.

What if my mother passed away neglected while I was chasing my dreams? What if my daughter's future got ruined because I didn't pay enough attention to her health? What if my son learns about the surrogacy in my absence and resents me for not carrying him and not being present after he was born? What if my friends abandon me due to my changing priorities? What if I land up old and alone? What if I resent myself for giving up my purpose? So, I did it all, spread myself thin.

The pressures screamed, old patterns started to possess my mind – be a good mother, daughter, wife, friend. But this time, I listened to my inner voice, the voice that belonged to my soul.

That deep voice of my inner wisdom knew exactly how much I could stretch to hold it all compassionately – myself and the demands from life that I was faced with.

The one time in my life when no one felt let down was when I didn't let myself down. In hindsight, I see how the power of perspective granted me the poise to make choices that served others and me.

Give up or hold on?

There were moments that tempted me to drop it all back down. The journey often felt too heavy. Self-doubt would overshadow my strengths, whispering about my incapabilities and suggesting I should shrink back to safety, scaring me that I didn't have the endurance to face the storms.

It had only been three months since my mom's passing. I was still so fragile and nowhere near finding my own. I had my final exam of my final year waiting for me and I had only two options: to give the exam and get done with my Master's programme or delay it by a whole year. I was exhausted, confused, grief-stricken, asthmatic, anxious and very worried for my daughter. Her scoliosis was rapidly worsening. The hump on her back was a big signboard that stared at me every day and screamed "GIVE UP". So, I told myself that I should push my exam by a year, grieve my mom's passing, get my daughter's surgery done, prove to my son that I am an awesome mom, take the year to recover and then give my exam.

The moment I made this decision, my companion anxiety roared louder instead of calming. My body seemed to be wiser than my mind this time around. Was it pushing me to give up or give IN? Could it be telling me to hold on tight, dig deeper, honour myself and stay committed to my purpose?

Anxiety can be dark and scary. It brings up fear and feelings of doom. We may feel a complete loss of control. But what it truly wants might be for us to grab back control and beat the uncertainty. The more control we lose fighting unseen threats and the more powerless we feel, the louder anxiety can scream. Therefore, imagining presumed dangers can create a false sense of certainty and control even if the anticipation is 'doom'. I felt trapped struggling in this painful whirlpool. During this time, I was angry with God and my Guru – my faith shaken and my anchor broken.

It is only when I turned back to my spiritual path and combined it with intensive counselling therapy that my mind started slowing down. I rediscovered strength and resilience. My anxiety started calming down and I could think more clearly.

I realised that giving up was not an option and I had to get through. There was light waiting for me at the end of this tunnel. The woman who raised me deserved more than dishonour. She taught me to persist through storms and keep going. My daughter needed to see her mother courageously carry on too. I couldn't let hardship break me.

The light ahead was calling out to me and my dream was fuelled again. With one-pointed focus, I funnelled everything into my studies, my health practices, and leaned on my most steadfast supporters, my biggest strengths even today, while some sceptical friends fell away.

But crisis revealed who would ride with me through the fire.

Beginning to the end

One day before my last exam, my blood pressure fell and I fainted in the morning. The doctor told me I needed to get admitted immediately. I refused. I requested to get treated at home instead. I drew energy from an IV in my arm and strength from some deeper will, proving to myself that 'I CAN' and scored a distinction.

I look back to understand – anxiety emerges when we feel helpless. With faith in our inner power, faith in the divine power and surrender to the rhythm of our breath, in the here and now, we are never helpless. If we lean into loving support and spiritual connection, we can recognise the powerful life force flowing through us. It is unbreakable and stronger than any grief, exhaustion or resistance seeking to suffocate us.

Why Mrs India?

As a counselling psychologist, I had found my purpose. I felt complete and helping others embodied my ikigai. My ikigai lay in marrying my passion, talents, and profession with my vision to spread mental-health awareness.

I felt so full and had so much to give. I yearned for a bigger platform to broadcast that message more widely. At the same time, the ex-model in me who missed the glitz of that world encouraged me to dive in and enrol for the pageant.

Nervous excitement stirred into self-doubt. Was I too old? Would my children feel proud or embarrassed? My old doubts came back to the forefront – fear of failure resurfaced, old wounds of ridicule and pain came up. The idea of the spotlight suddenly felt too blinding.

The internal drama took centre stage but this time, I worked through it with self-love and empathy rather than criticism. I was connected deeply to my purpose, the choice felt clearer making it easy to lean into growth over comfort.

I got through the different stages of the audition. Selected as a finalist, I invested fully in my transformation, surrounding myself with experts and disciplines to shine even brighter. I started reading up on current affairs, I focused on my mental health, did my spiritual practice in a disciplined way, left no stone unturned when it came to my nutrition and physical exercise. I took care of my hair and skin. I went back to my speech therapist to finetune the rough edges again, as my stammering had come up again due to the nervousness of being on stage under the spotlight for the pageant. I worked with a voice-crafting expert. Grooming, styling, ramp walking, personality development, and hair and makeup tutorials were all part of my training process.

Win or lose, I already felt victorious. My fear of both failure and success fell away as I stepped boldly into my power and light once more. Purpose took over as I now worked towards embodying everything the crown stood for. I felt ready to inspire others to claim their voice and dreams.

Victory is inevitable – crown or no crown

I felt almost rescued from the bondage of fears – failure and success. I discovered my capacity to put in all my energy into something without obsessing about the end goal. I relished my journey one hydrating sip at a time.

Investing fully in myself and my passions without being

obsessively attached to outcomes allowed me to flourish. The destination mattered but I also had so many roses to smell on the road leading up to it. Each moment passes without return and with it goes away its precious fragrance.

My resilience tenaciously persisting through grief to take my exams enabled me to stand confidently as a counselling psychologist on that stage. Without that strength, born through adversity, or my supporters, my loved ones and my Guru steadfastly behind me, the crown may never have found my head.

Before this, I rebounded between co-dependence and extreme independence struggling to stumble on self-worth. I eventually slipped into interdependency, supported by my mentors and cheerleaders. They held me accountable while empowering my voice. Humans blossom best in interdependence – I alone could not sustain the heaviness of life and required a nurturing community too.

The crown merely topped my long-held dreams now achieved. My journey gave more than a title – it taught me to embrace the process, enjoy the present moment and not just the outcome. Learning to value impermanence and the surprises that uncertainty holds are the true jewels that I received along the way. These lessons painstakingly learnt are more precious than any glittering ornament placed only briefly on my head before passing to the next bearer. These lessons forever embellished within my soul bloom within me.

Inner demons arrive on the runway

Time management was the biggest challenge I faced during

my pageant training. Juggling parenting, work and a rigorous training routine pulled me in endless directions. My young son, a daughter needing therapy, and clients relying on me needed me to balance my time and be extremely disciplined.

In the beginning I found myself scrambling reactively, until I took some time to proactively plan. I took to pen on paper and scheduled my day before I went to bed and ran through it in the morning every day so that I wouldn't miss out on anything. I also made sure I did my breathwork and meditation every single day. So, while I continued running from pillar to post, at least I wasn't a headless chicken.

I knew exactly where I was going.

Discipline and order calmed the chaos yet kept the energy high.

The chaos outside was no match for the composure that I had cultivated inside through many years of storms.

I was in the rhythm of the breath and flow that my discipline demanded. I had it all figured out with my anxiety in check. But my momentum got derailed and I was struck by fear like a lightning storm. My little bean's impending spinal surgery could not be avoided. I had to come out from under the duvet of discipline that I had created. Anxiety was waiting for me like a demon ready to paw. I found it very hard to sit still and meditate so I just did my breathwork instead. My body was finding it very hard to cope with the emotional turmoil. All I could think about was my daughter's spine and the knife cutting through my daughter's back.

The disciplined routine that had anchored me was suddenly

futile and inefficient.

I coped by numbing the internal wreckage with tubs of ice-cream. I was unable to peel myself away from my daughter's side in our last weeks before the operation. My body and spirit were crouching down, dreading the trauma ahead.

To the outside eye, I maintained my brave face standing strong and solid. But inwardly I was crumbling into pieces. I wanted to flee this nightmare or fast-forward into the future. My lifelong battle with anxiety was amplified to the hilt built with fears for my little girl – my beating heart.

My daughter, my little bean, kept me focused. She believed in me enough for the both of us when I faltered. Her relentless reminders of my pageant dreams transmuted my terror back into purposeful preparation.

By grace, her surgery was a success and her recovery was a breeze.

And that propelled me towards my goal with fresh gusto and bursting with energy.

What now?

Winning the crown transformed life in some ways. My inner child felt the satisfaction, joy, and gratitude of a fulfilled dream. Euphoria is fleeting when it is not joined to an aim. After the celebrations ended, I was seated in a crowded room of sadness and confusion.

I had intently focused on this achievement and then realised the title alone could not fulfil me. I continued to feel lonely and directionless, only now I had a sparkling accessory on my head.

I was not the one to be satisfied by fleeting glory and my win felt empty, lacking deeper purpose. I had lost my vision and chased external distractions, abandoning my inner truth.

I still felt hollow and directionless, more than ever despite adoring the glittering crown I had yearned for. I had made the mistake of confusing external validation with inner purpose. The driving force of my singular goal had now been struck off; I was centrally located in an empty void – what now?

After much introspection, I realised the genuine intent and went back to my core drivers – healing, service, and human connection. These hold value that no trophies and crowns can. It is only my inner royalty that could align to my intrinsic passions of empowerment and understanding others.

I wanted to heal myself and touch the lives around me.

The gift of surrender

My journey has given me a beautiful gift and deeply imprinted this lesson: the gift of the present moment and the beautiful lesson of surrender. We always have choice in the present moment; outcomes may remain beyond our grasp but choices, well within. Being able to surrender is one of my biggest strengths and the wisdom that comes with it grants me immense freedom and power.

I can wholeheartedly work towards dreams with the awareness that life may derail me down unexpected avenues. Alignment lies in flowing, swaying with the moment of the tide and allowing destiny to present itself. Fighting the inevitable only breeds suffering.

Surrender has not only freed me but it has also given

me a sense of control in a strange way. By accepting that I cannot control all pieces of life's puzzle, my locus of control simplifies by encouraging conscious acceptance.

Surrender strengthens my muscle of faith. All it takes is to release redundant beliefs and expectations with awareness. This process of letting go lightens my load enormously, automatically creating free space for relaxation and by freeing the bandwidth that was previously occupied by anxiety.

An open palm holds infinity as compared to a closed fist.

I mindfully connect to the golden words, "It is what it is".

Surrender – give up or give in?

Many situations in my life have brought me to my knees, made me beg to the unseen and eventually forced me to give up and feel like a failure through this process.

But the resurrection has occurred only when I learnt the art of surrender and understood the power that downfalls held.

That it has the power to transform me and reconstruct my foundation and rebirth a new me.

The mind fights for control, believing it ensures safety and happiness. So, when life destabilises us, trauma responses like fight-or-flight take over – driven by fear to regain footing. These subconscious strategies are depleting and self-defeating.

I reached a point where I had nothing left in my body, mind, or soul to fight anymore. All my resources and strategies had depleted and that is the point where I found gold. My fatigue slipped into this gorgeous pot of gold called surrender. For me surrender happened when I was left with nothing to happen.

I was ready to let go and give in but I was still not ready to give up.

When this state took over me, I embraced it. Nothing really changed instantly, but what changed was my state of mind. I did not take shelter in my trauma responses. I started feeling a sense of calm that only surrender could provide.

The mystery

Surrender seems paradoxical – the mystery of surrender is that letting go creates opportunities for fuller investment. I am able to relax my tight grip on control yet I can focus on wise effort towards goals. I plan more strategically but hold plans loosely. It gives me the space to allow destiny to surprise me – some gifts unimaginably miraculous. I have learnt to meet worry with curiosity over fear at most times.

Surrender grants me four diamond studded pillars – faith, grace, gratitude, and access to greater wisdom. By acknowledging my strengths and my limits, I am able to call upon higher support to guide and protect me, easing the burden of my "not-so-delicate" shoulders. Surrendering the compulsion to control and squeeze tight keeps my hands open to receive abundantly.

Faith replaces fear.

Trust replaces uncertainty.

Ease replaces clutching.

Surrender replaces crumbling.

Confidence and self-esteem – unimaginable dreams

Both my Master's and Mrs India journeys felt impossible at times. On multiple occasions, I needed to prioritise people and situations around me – which I had done many times in my life.

My need to reclaim my power was non-negotiable and I refused to give in to the old traps this time. The seemingly unsurmountable power of trauma was not going to control my choices. Trauma, after all, had taught me that diminishing myself helps no one but only shrinks me. By standing tall through the fire, with divine grace and tremendous self-work, I modelled resilience.

Gratitude is the mother of all. Today, in my eyes it overwhelms everything. It anchored me when my world collapsed, and it granted me this healing platform to lift others.

I look myself in the eye with deep love now, like a mother for her baby and a child for her mother. I found a newfound romance with myself flowing with forgiveness and gratitude.

I am so proud of myself for all that I have achieved. I am still fragile, broken, wounded, sometimes even afraid but I am so proud of everything I have become and everything I am becoming while I am not ashamed of my vulnerabilities.

I survived, I became – I celebrate

Confidence has replaced doubt. My Master's, my crown and all the obstacles have stirred in me an unspoken knowing – I am capable and life always had my back, even when I failed to trust it.

The generosity of life through all my ups and downs has given me a sense of boldness. The courage to dream bigger, love harder, and embrace uncertainty, is the ocean for miracles.

This unseen force with its invisible momentum will carry me on its magnificent wings again. I got me here – I made it here. I can make it anywhere my wings dare to take me.

And life nods, affirming: You've got this, your highness!

Thoughts = reality – wisdom?

Life bombarded me with avalanches during phases of my journey, as it does to most of us. Each crushing blow feeling inhuman and impossible to overcome threatened to bury me. I emerged realising that my perception is governed by my thoughts. My thoughts and my beliefs dictate how I view hardship. Where my mind goes, energy flows. My perception determines the power a person or situation has over me. It determines whether I feel defeated or strengthened.

I witnessed that my beliefs are the operating system of my thoughts. They play a vital role in how we frame our challenges. My old wounds got triggered by thoughts indicating a lack of safety, failure and abandonment. On the other hand, thoughts that were aligned with my goals gave me hope, strength and direction.

It's beautiful to believe that focus flows from assumptions. Assumption can be the root of manifestation. What occupied my consciousness manifested. My thoughts of insufficiency and lack gave birth to a reality that was scarce and unfulfilling. My thoughts that assumed life's support despite setbacks opened up focus, vigour and abundance.

Yet thoughts cannot always be controlled. Through meditation, I learnt to observe them without judgement or engagement. I was able to slow my thoughts down, creating space between reaction and response. These gaps were the filters to negative, self-defeating thoughts. Slowing my breath calmed my racing mind, bringing awareness to replace the unhealthy stories playing on loop. I was able to examine my limited narratives and redirect them to focused self-serving pathways. From this serene vantage point, I was able to release thoughts that depleted me and nurture a growth mindset.

And I achieved focus, clarity, and discipline through breathwork, meditation and healthy cognitive self-talk. The wise ones often say that focus and discipline are the highest form of self-love. I would like to add that focus and discipline are the most loving way to achieve anything you want and almost everything is possible.

I always find happiness when I am focused on the larger goal. That's the vision element of my ikigai – the one that drove me to take part in Mrs India. I feel deeply happy when I see people heal and find their happiness and this for me is my macro goal while my micro goal is to be completely connected to myself. It is only when I am well-established in my micro goal can my vision be fulfilled.

But everything I am and everything I do is rooted in my unshakeable faith in the divine.

Diving into the self

1. Do you find yourself fearing failure or success? How

does this fear manifest in your life?

2. If so, in what ways is this fear limiting your potential?

3. How significant is external validation in shaping your thoughts, beliefs and actions?

4. How does your fear of judgement affect your willingness to pursue your dreams?

5. Are you sacrificing your authentic self to gain acceptance or validation from others and how can you use self-compassion to counteract the need?

6. What practices can help you embrace the art of surrender?

7. What is your overarching sense of purpose, and how does it guide your life?

8. What steps can you take to align your daily actions with your larger sense of purpose?

9. Identify activities, causes, or pursuits that resonate with and ignite your sense of purpose.

10. How can embracing vulnerability help you grow personally and professionally?

Surrender is paradoxical. It liberates, but grants profound control rooted in the wisdom of conscious acceptance.

Uncovering My Mindscape

Manifesting My Truth

Life presents us with ever so many situations. Along with the beautiful feelings, we may also feel betrayed, let down, cheated, abandoned, unheard, lonely, and the like. These emotions can evoke feelings of anger, resentment, sadness, revenge, disappointment, hurt, and even aggression. As a result, we may express these emotions through external reactions like aggression or passive behaviours like crying, oversharing, sleeplessness, changes in appetite, sadness or depression, anxiety, and more. These unhealthy responses to our feelings and emotions can have a profound impact on our mental, physical, and spiritual wellbeing. Unprocessed feelings may hamper the clarity in our communication, both with the self and others, affecting our overall life. I've personally experienced this cyclical pattern multiple times in my life, and each time it's left me feeling lost and aweigh. Through my vulnerability and personal stories, I hope to illustrate that emotional suffering when left unaddressed can give rise to deeper hurts and fears. These hurts and fears then form unhealthy patterns, which may loop us in without awareness.

How forgiveness healed my life and relationships

Forgiveness has an intense yet sincere power. My entire being felt the lightness of a feather when I permitted forgiveness to penetrate me and take over. I recently stumbled upon a commanding quote that really resonated with me: "Resentment is like drinking poison and expecting the enemy to die." This simmering poison will only boil over, making us sick, cause us to suffer, damage our relationships, and suppress our happiness, joy, success, and overall growth. As I reflected on these words, my inner victim rebelled; she had thrived on the comfort of blame and loved to nurse resentment. I realised that this only conserves the cycle of suffering and sinks us down in guilt, remorse, and even shame.

This profound power of forgiveness – both towards others and ourselves – is an integral step in breaking free from this self-defeating cycle. But the thing about forgiveness is, it's very subtle. It doesn't come from willpower or self-discipline, but rather from a place of heartfelt vulnerability and surrender.

Forgiveness comes through understanding the root causes of our resentment and asserting an internal locus of control through prayer, faith and surrender. It is then that we can begin to heal the wounds within ourselves. Every trigger points to a place within us that needs healing. Letting go of the past and embracing the present with grace and renewed purpose is the liberating gift of sincere forgiveness.

My mother spent her entire life trying to teach me the value of forgiveness and I worked so hard to be disciplined about instilling it within me. But I struggled to internalise it. The obedient daughter within me would often justify and rationalise the actions of others to the point where I shadowed my own feelings and emotions. I became increasingly passive, uncommunicative, and sought validation with desperation. In my conditional attempt to forgive, passive-aggression became my modus operandi. I was stuck in a cycle of justifying misdeeds, neglecting my own needs, and then pining for validation, all in the name of forgiveness. I thought I was being kind and compassionate, but in reality, I was secretly hoarding resentment. This self-inflicted burden only caused more harm to myself and others. It served to further shrink my own being far away from myself and my authenticity.

My poor mother tried her best to explain, but I never truly understood the concept of forgiveness. It was when I touched rock bottom and took a hard hit that I realised I had been living a lie. As an adult, I now see that I relished the beautiful flavour of forgiveness only when I took responsibility for my own healing and growth. Forgiveness is not about ignoring or enabling the actions of others. My past remains unchanged; a child might be too nice to understand the ever so complex yet sincere simplicity of forgiveness. Today, I cannot change the past, but I have the power to choose how I respond to it. My childhood trauma may have shaped me, but I am determined to stay on my path of self-discovery and embrace a healthier, more authentic way of living.

I slowly came to realise that I had consumed so much poison of anger and resentment that my body was suffering from persistent headaches and gut issues, and my mind was in complete chaos. I was desperate to silence my mind and find some peace and quiet but no amount of meditation seemed to help. I was also desperate to restore my physical health, but no matter how nutritious my diet was or how much I exercised, my body remained unresponsive.

Life had brought me to my knees, and I was stumped in despair. I needed help to resurrect and in my hour of need, I turned to my mental-health therapist for help. After a long and intense session of venting my frustrations, my therapist did something unexpected – she sat in silence and gave me the space to let it all out. When I was finally done, she asked me two simple yet profound questions:

"Does forgiveness mean sweeping misdeeds under the rug?"

"Does forgiveness mean only forgiving others?"

After which, she sent me home with instructions to return only when I had found the answers.

With a lot of help from my therapist and my spiritual practice, my journey began. It unblocked an abundant flow of self-forgiveness, the ripples of which overflow into my world as compassion, kindness and pure love for myself and others. For when I grant myself grace, I can extend the same towards others.

This laborious and hard-won self-love qualifies me to love wholly. I am able to respect boundaries yet give and receive freely without depleting myself or others. Assertive communication gently conveys truth minus anger and with minimum conflict. I comfort my inner child like a mother and make peace with the past. I only used the survival mechanisms I knew and understood. Passive-aggression may have once served me but now I recognise it as a limitation to my growth.

I have learnt to observe my mind's chatter like a mother watches her child with unadulterated self-love, compassion and empathy. For a mother, forgiving her child is not even a matter of thought, as a mother accepts her child with unconditional love and acceptance. This is the unquestioning love my mother modelled through her relentlessness to hold me and lift me. Finally, the seeds of my mother's relentless compassionate efforts bore sweet, sweet fruits.

My body was healing – the gut was getting better and headaches dissolving as anxieties began relaxing.

As I started forgiving myself, all the passive resentment and anger I was holding towards others and my environment eventually started dropping on its own like a domino effect.

The light shines through me again as I befriend my darkness with kindness.

I recover by inviting every broken piece back where it belongs – home to THE SELF.

When perspective meets forgiveness

I found that learning the true art of forgiveness most definitely changed my perspective towards myself and then towards the environment and the people in my environment by default.

I realised it does not mean holding on to toxic relationships or excusing misconduct. It means accepting the person, people or situation for what they are; understanding the impact of their behaviour or the environment on oneself; and making healthy choices for oneself by choosing to not drink the poison of resentment or anger because that is only harming one person, the most important person – YOU.

I do not justify breach of boundaries or betrayal. I acknowledge the behaviour's impact on me and make choices honouring my wellbeing. This means that I gently create distance with the person or the environment without harbouring resentment.

I choose peace and healing for my own wellbeing and strictly not allowing any perpetrators to come into my most precious home – ME.

In that way, forgiveness is so beautifully paradoxical – so selfish yet so infinitely selfless.

It's also a journey, a winding road of ease and unease. Some days empathy comes easily; other times the pain and the anger are hanging on with all their might, making the release even harder. I've found ease in accepting the fluctuating range of my emotions with compassion rather than judging them. When I'm gripped by painful emotions, I've found that widening the lens of perspective by simply acknowledging it and not gabbing on keeps the suffering from perpetuating.

My peace is my responsibility. Safeguarding myself and my healing by consolidating my energies to myself prevents my precious energy from dissipating. Blame and external focus causes our energy to leak and deplete while consolidating our energies to ourselves causes our energy to expand and accelerate healing. This is where the power of perspective comes in. We all have this superpower; we only need to learn to use it.

We heal in silence

The phrase "silence is golden" holds a lot of wisdom when understood correctly as we unfold its layers.

For a large part of my early life, I took recourse in silence. But this silence came from fear. I swallowed words and choked my emotions. My fear of shame or rejection was a grave cost to my spirit; it was poisonous. It shrunk me as a person, my dreams, desires, needs, my voice, and my being on the whole.

Then later in my life, the silence took another shape. I had given up on life and lost all hope. I was a prisoner to my silence and was trapped in it. My repressed emotions shouted within me, screaming and begging to be heard, while I placated and tried to please everyone externally. It began as self-preservation but eventually eroded my dreams and desires, until I entirely lost sight of and disconnected from my own needs.

Imprisoned shrieks noiselessly screaming in my head,

leading to inner chaos. This overwhelming inner chaos discharged as passive-aggression. The internal confusion clouded my mind and blurred my emotional vocabulary making passive-aggression my only choice of expression – I knew no better at the time.

My forced silence left me tragically voiceless and weak, not vulnerable and nobly strong.

In time, I discovered the extraordinary power of silence when chosen mindfully with wisdom. This stillness creates space to access thoughts, connect with one's feelings and emotions, check in with one's needs and desires, and reconnect with inner truth without judgement. The gentle inner whispers emerge to reveal what lies beneath in the deepest parts of our wonderful selves.

My healthy silence took me closer to my body, mind, and soul. It helped me become more self-aware and helped me get the validation I had looked for externally. It helped me feel seen by ME.

I started tapping into this silence more often for a few minutes a day and I discovered a stillness that was heavenly. I slowly started learning self-control and developing patience. As my self-awareness deepened, my purpose started unveiling itself to me and my focus and creativity got deeply enhanced.

I also found that when I was angry, uncomfortable, or dealing with unhealthy emotions, a few minutes of silence helped me transform my reactions into healthy responses.

There is a time to listen and a time to speak

Silence in itself is a powerful response. In moments of

grief or conflict, silence speaks more than words. It can be a protection from the wounds of some words. Profound acceptance and self-reflection can come through silence and protection from the daggers of impulsive argument. I have found that pausing protects me too – from reacting thoughtlessly on impulse. It, in fact, makes space for wisdom to guide me by bringing a centred coolness to my fiery emotions. I have learnt not to react when the fire of my emotions is burning. Silence, in its divine form, is connection that transcends silence as avoidance. Empathetic listening through mindful pauses in an argument or disagreement dissolves the divisive barriers of "you" and "I" and merges it into the oneness of "us".

Silence helps me retain my power. It protects me from regret, helps me slow my thoughts down, creates time and space to reflect on my words and choose healthy respectful modes of communication. If someone remains closed, I choose to simply retrieve my peace without taking offense. My power is retained because I can choose how much of myself I want to give away and how vulnerable I would like to be with the other person. I reflect on questions like, "How safe do I feel to express my anger?", "Am I going to feel heard and respected?", "Do I have the emotional, mental and physical strength to work on conflict resolution at the moment?", "Do I have the capacity to listen and understand this moment?" It unfolds my personal power of perspective both towards myself and the other person's point of view. I choose when and what to speak, I choose to be vulnerable or not, and I choose to uplift or remove myself from conversations that won't do me any good.

This not the powerlessness but the POWER of silence.

Peeling the layers and diving deeper into silence

At the deepest level, I lost my need to seek validation. It helped me understand that I do not owe any explanations to anyone. The only eyes that validate me are the ones I see in my reflection. My silence gave me the power of stronger and more effective communication. It has taught me to set and respect my boundaries while it has also taught people to respect my boundaries.

Once my fearful escape, now silence is like my trusted ally. I respond thoughtfully not impulsively.

My silence has healed my deepest layers and continues to do so. It is teaching me to face the world and not escape from it. It patiently waits by my side to embrace me warmly like a comforting mother waiting faithfully should I need a soothing refuge within myself.

Stillness and silence: a daily practice

Silence is a skill that can be mastered through practice. My meditation helps me maintain a peaceful inner sanctuary. My daily quiet time keeps me aligned with this profound peace that rests so beautifully at the centre of my soul.

Silence has many friends: breathwork, art, reading, music, dance, nature, exercise, yoga, journalling or enjoying that splendid cup of coffee in the early hours of the day or the quiet hours before dusk.

All these help regulate emotions, promote patience and

allow things to pass.

And through all this, the beauty is that the pandemonium of the external rarely possesses the power to unsettle the internal. It is through silence only that the noise can truly be enjoyed.

Gossip to cancel – should complicit culture be implicated?

On a chirpy Sunday evening, I walked into my daughter's room to overhear a young girl announcing with pride that she had gotten her classmate to leave the school. This friend of my daughter had ganged up with a bunch of girls and ostracised her. "We cancelled her!" she reported with glee. She was completely oblivious to the reality of what she had done and the grave impact it may have on the other girl's life for years to come.

I looked at the young girls, triggered, my disbelief thickly layering my face. Cruel ruthlessness was being treated as a casual sport. "Cancel culture" had trickled down from the starry celebrities who faced public liabilities for wrongdoings or distorted judgement to condemning little children and cornering them into isolation. "Cancelling", slandering, blackening, shaming and shunning someone through mass bullying and smear campaigns without any humanity or consideration of the damage crushed my heart.

I have found myself a victim of gossip and cancel culture since I was a little kid. I stammered, I got gossiped about, shamed, humiliated, bullied and cancelled out. I rebelled, but through passive-aggression and unhealthy silence because I was so gravely dismissed and cancelled. Either I was treated as invisible or I got gossiped about and cancelled further. I was stuck in a lonely painful vicious cycle where isolation was my only friend.

I then went on to become a successful model. I got featured in magazines, plastered on billboards and walked the ramp for luxurious lifestyle fashion shows, despite the haunting voices of the bullies mumbling dark whispers of self-doubt through it all. These thugs from my past life then changed course. They wanted to embrace me. I propelled back into safety as old wounds reopened making the dark murmurs turn into loud painful shrieks. They didn't want me for me, they wanted me for my accolades. I was still scared of the violators who yet again hounded me ruthlessly – this time adorned in sheep's clothing.

As I grew up, I did experience "cancellation" through different stages of my life. Bullies seem to have a consistent pattern whether they are teenagers or adults in their midlife. I grew past the thugs eventually. I no longer needed external validation and the dark murmurs had changed to gentle compassionate divine whispers. Whispers emitting the divine sound of love and support. When I entered Mrs India pursuing my long-held dreams, I just wanted to become my best version. I wanted everything it took to reach my own highest self. I did come out a winner and the naysayers were busy doing what they do best – focused on others and hiding from their inner selves.

Unstable as they are, their fickle minds now hurried around me to praise me. This time, though, they had no power. No power to trigger me and no power to elevate me.

Neither their praise nor their criticism means anything.

Gossip, cancel culture and smear campaigns are the most lethal poisons there may be. This poison when swallowed is made up of depression, suicidal thoughts, intrusive thoughts, self-harm, eating disorders, anxiety and a Pandora's box of more and more darkness. The main ingredient of this potent slow killer is loneliness. Passive participation and listening to gossip are as bad as gossiping. It has the power to destroy a person to the point of no return.

When my triggers settled and I created space for my rational mind to take the front seat, I decided to speak with my daughter. I patiently explained to my daughter that, for her generation, bullying shows up on a public platform through a tiny screen. The lethal power of this little screen can be tremendous and information dispatched through it can travel at the speed of lightning and go viral. Unfortunately, it is never forgotten and never deleted from the cloud of growing technology.

I taught my daughter the great power of the "pause". When the impulse to gossip strikes, pause, breathe, pause, breathe, and repeat till it passes.

My mother used to tell me: "If you don't have anything nice to say, don't say it at all."

Break the mould, make your own fit

We are all taught through conditioning, media, society, culture, religion, gender bias and so on that each one of us belongs to a particular mould. Most of us spend our lives trying to fit into this mould. And when we don't fit, we may have to face unnerving opinions. Opinions are like these pre-decided moulds. We have to change the way we behave in order to be seen and accepted. We create versions of ourselves we think will fit. In the process of trying to reduce the gap between ourselves and someone else's opinions, we may widen the gap with our authentic inner selves. We hope that these unauthentic versions of ourselves will be loved and accepted. But do others ever accept our unauthentic version? Do they acknowledge that we are shrinking just to fit into their mould?

Let's begin by checking in with ourselves first.

Who am I?

What does my mould look like?

Do I even have a mould I'd like to fit into?

Why do I want to shrink myself for an opinion from others?

What makes my light shine infinitely?

Allowing myself to shine infinitely

Cancellation is part of most of our lives through some stage or the other. Gossip and cancellation may not be in our control but resurrection is. How we handle the cancellation and our rise post-cancellation remains our choice and the power we flaunt. With fierce unconditional self-love and a bold self-acceptance of the whole self, one doesn't need to add self-inflicted cancellation to the pre-existing complex societal mix.

I am burnt out with the fatigue of putting on a façade of strength and perfection. I never again wish to be called strong. Instead, I want to let my guard down, be loved, and feel supported and understood. I give myself permission to let my guard down. Strength, self-love, self-care and self-acceptance innately reside inside of me. The divinity of their true nature will always remain untouched by the adulterations of the world and they don't thrive in the hardened shell. They sit in my core, yielding their expansive light, and I can dive into their soothing solitude whenever I require rest, realignment and rejuvenation. In that sweet surrender lies the holy nectar of the self.

Power and responsibility go hand-in-hand. One thrives on the other. Victimhood, blame and external validation is an endless blackhole, perpetually draining us of our spiritedness and vitality. I refuse to fit into redundant moulds that limit me in boxes. I choose to liberate myself from the pressure of shrinking to keep this archaic system going. "The good girl", "the duty-bound girl", "the perfect woman" – God forbid she make one mistake and breathe outside of her predefined stifling "true" identity!

Who taught me victimhood? Who taught me perfection? I can't even seem to recall the first whisper. I question these voices – they do not know what they talk of!

As I release these chains of confinement, question inherent expectations, and break the mould to shine infinitely, I reclaim my personal authority.

I spring free as nature intended, and I root myself into my

own beliefs and spread the aromatic essence of the flower that I'm meant to bloom into.

Diving into the self

1. Make a list of past grievances or resentments you are still holding on to.

2. How do these grievances affect your emotional wellbeing and overall quality of life?

3. What steps can you take to begin the journey toward forgiveness?

4. How can you view forgiveness as a gift to yourself rather than as a concession to those who have hurt you?

5. Do you believe that integrating moments of silence and stillness into your daily routine can foster introspection, self-reflection, and a connection with your inner wisdom, and why?

6. Which practices, such as meditation, deep breathing, or mindful solitude, align with your personal needs and preferences?

7. How can you make them a discipline?

8. How can you cultivate unconditional self-love and acceptance to protect yourself from the negative effects of gossip and cancel culture?

9. What personal or societal norms would you like to challenge or change to let your light shine more brightly?

10. How can you identify and release the emotional blocks that prevent you from moving forward?

Self-worth is the shield against gossip and cancel culture, turning exclusion into inclusion. Its power is rooted in the 'self' and not in the measurement of the worth.

Lonely to Alone

Peace Within Solitude

My story has always been about standing solo.

I chose to stand solo because of my speech difficulties, I chose to stand solo because of the rejection, humiliation and impatience that came every single time I needed to use my voice and be heard. It would all become about the stutter – my handicap – not what I needed or what I wanted to say. I was the clown of my class and every morning going to school was trauma.

I grew up in an apartment building with 14 kids and made only one real friend, Sean. Sean got me. He teased me when I stuttered but he wanted to listen to what I was saying. He wanted to understand, he wanted to make me stronger, and be there for me in his own childlike way. When I look back today, I have so much to thank Sean for. He doesn't even know what he did for that lonely girl who spent her whole life hiding. He was there for me and he believed in me.

I ended up playing sports with the slum-dwellers' kids across my building. They accepted me unconditionally and some of them even admired me. Occasionally, Sean joined me and I felt safe. One learns to find one's own means to survive and, now that I think about it, that part of my childhood keeps me grounded even today.

Sean lives on another continent today but he still lives in a big part of my heart.

As far as school goes, every time I stood up to read that chapter in English class, I was standing solo again, naked with my ugliness, handicap, and vulnerability on display as the audience would scowl and mock, waiting impatiently for this show to come to an end. The girls were too embarrassed to be my friend and the boys were too embarrassed to date me.

The school bus was the biggest circus. The saga with the perversive monster started there. But when I found my voice, he regretted it because I found him and beat the puny, pitted-face pervert on a public street... solo!

There's a lack of sensitivity that pervades our society. This insensitivity needs to be addressed for people who struggle in their own skin. Instead of being made to feel safe and heard, they are instead reduced to a coffee-table conversation, laughed at, abandoned and left only to be forgotten.

I gave up dreams and opportunities because of my speech difficulties. My speech disfluency bred not only my external judgement and self-shame but an inner critic too – my fear of failure. The humiliation that came with stuttering made perfectionism an obsession for me. And if I didn't match up to my own uncompromising standards, I chose to be lonely. Isolation eventually became a subconscious habit. Isolation was seemingly safer than repeated exposure. I may have escaped the risk of mockery and falling short, but I manufactured a larger danger. I shrunk myself down to zero and completely abandoned myself – leaving my little heart to survive alone.

I resented the abandonment. I resented both, my peers and my own potential. The toxicity was metastatic and over time percolated into my entire world. I rebelled against the very same worlds I hid from. I punished society and in turn punished myself through rejection. My fear of judgement manifested as judging others harshly first.

I spun into a vicious cycle of blame. Blaming others fuelled my loneliness but it protected me from the feeling that "I didn't belong", until grace helped me change.

The illusion of perfection

In truth, these unrelenting standards of perfection that I chased did gift me grit. I worked very, very hard to fix my speech and gave myself no break. It worked but I didn't know where to draw the line and I lost me in the process.

I achieved it all. I became a successful ramp model, and the same people who shied away from me now took pride in saying they watched me grow up. As I have matured, I have come to understand that a lot of people aren't inherently mean. They are mean because they are probably hiding from themselves – running away from their own reflection. Sometimes they don't know what to do, how to empathise, how to be compassionate and how to love.

We are never really taught compassion as children; what we are truly taught is survival. We are taught to toughen up and come out on top in most cases, neglecting compassion – compassion for others and even for ourselves. We are never really taught balance – the skill to walk on that tight rope that sits right at the epicentre of the spectrum, between compassion and survival.

Today I understand that those unrelenting standards that I chased came from my need to prove my worth to myself and not to anyone else. I defined my self-worth based on every battle I won and every piece of validation I received.

Mistaking achievement for self-esteem, I grasped for visible validation of my talents.

I have poured myself abundantly into others for so long. I have learnt to become my own safe space. My healing has filled me with so much empathy, compassion and love to offer. But what I'm learning today is also pivotal in my growth: to stop struggling, to open my hands, and TO RECEIVE without resistance, guilt or minimising my worth.

Existential loneliness

I always felt very alone. I think I suffered from existential loneliness. I feel maybe existential loneliness is a part of me.

It is a feeling of fundamental separateness from the world around.

My stammer made me feel like I was the only person in the world who had a speech disfluency. It was the world against me. The laughter and the impatience made me hold myself back and hide from my feelings. Because if I felt them, I would have to express them. Hence, best not to address any feelings and become numb by choosing indifference. It was my most effective safety net. I was very sensitive to rejection and was quick to pick it up. But I also overlooked red flags as quickly because even a little bit of love and acceptance was good enough for my poor personal standards.

What I did my entire life was to try to fix the external environment. I rejected myself for my own incompetencies. I felt humiliated by my own handicap and was ever so impatient with myself. These feelings made me feel lonely and made it harder to reach out when I needed people.

Today, I reach out to my selected people. These people are my core group and hold a large piece of my heart. I love them deeply but I still tend to get lost in solitude. I need to remind myself that I need my interpersonal relationships to break out of my inner world and into the external world.

I'm still working on breaking my old habit. I need to keep a check on my own imposturous voice that whispers at the back of my head that I will stammer if I speak and make a fool of myself again. I do not want to confirm my negativity bias and I tend to stay in a state of constant hypervigilance when I'm speaking. But my life changed when I truly learnt to accept the fearful voice and observe it from a distance. I embraced my speech – I may stammer even today but I'm not afraid of it.

So what if I stammer? So what if I break to consciously breathe when a word gets stuck? So what if someone walks away while I'm speaking? I welcomed my speech, embraced my life experiences that got me to stammer, comforted the girl in me who worked relentlessly to beat the stammer, and I OWN the woman in me who has had the courage to accept me with unconditional love and gratitude.

The biggest fear is the fear of fear itself, said Franklin D. Roosevelt. Today, I reach out to my selected people as and when I need. But I also remind myself that I need my interpersonal relationships as well.

Choosing solitude over loneliness

Loneliness is a state of mind and walks side-by-side through every transitional stage in life. The newborn baby may feel lonely because their cry may not be understood; the teenager may feel lonely because parents may not understand their rapidly changing hormones; the new mother may feel lonely because she feels overburdened and confused; the man may feel lonely because he's carrying the weight of the world on his shoulders; the CEO of the multinational may feel lonely as he watches his employees catch a drink in the evening without him, and so on. Divorce, changing locations, financial burdens, death, grief, etc., all lie under the shadows of loneliness.

Our inner void seeks completion through external relationships. The inner emptiness may constantly be on a hunt but may never really feel full.

As children, our happiness depends on the collection of our friends. The teenager feels a sense of belonging based on their popularity and accolades. Then, we look for romance and companionship to find meaning and later our life purpose is dependent on our children. And when they eventually fly off, we are left with an empty nest.

We are constantly looking. What are we looking for? Meaning? Purpose? Significance? Happiness? Contentment?

We look for these values outside of us. But true fulfilment only lies within the crux of our being. It shines bright when we go within and learn to rest within the stillness that lies at the depths of this vast ocean – THE SELF. And this is solitude.

Finding my best friend, within

Loneliness is a state of mind. It boils down to one's relationship with oneself. There is a vast difference between loneliness and solitude. Loneliness come with sadness and victimisation whereas solitude is a choice that involves engaging with the self through meaningful self-reflection.

Solitude is being able to enjoy our own company without escape through activity or people. Solitude entails a bliss and serenity that is untouched by the fleeting nature of our relationships. It is when we find our best friend within and build this relationship with ourselves that we strengthen our relationship with the world.

Embracing my brokenness within

Our relationship with the people in our lives, our relationship with the environment, our relationship with sleep, and our relationship with our habits simply mirrors our relationship with ourselves. We ingest the toxicity of shame by believing we are unworthy. This poison convinces us of our limitations and shortcomings. So, we hide from ourselves, we numb the pain, create the void, look for external validation as an antidote to this poison, settle for less and then poison ourselves further.

Consumption of this poison – in the form of shame, disrespect, lack of boundaries, verbal, sexual and physical abuse, drug abuse, alcoholism, excessive social media, guilt and so on – is a choice that we ourselves hold. Our instincts are our inbuilt protection and solid anchors that our soul gifts us. We are more inclined to consuming this poison when we don't trust ourselves and our instincts. But instead, we trust the approval and validation of external relationships. It is the distrust in our own capabilities that sows seeds of self-shame and self-doubt. We focus on our failures and imperfections and find it difficult to stand up to our needs. Therefore, we allow others to walk all over our boundaries and in turn feel a deep sense of loneliness because of self-abandonment.

Healing begins the moment we stop abandoning ourselves and start accepting ourselves. When we hold space for our brokenness within and allow the nectar of grace to flow out of the cracks.

This is where we realise our SELF-WORTH.

Unrealistic beauty standards – another pathway to loneliness

My mother struggled with vitiligo. She was agonised with the distinct white patches etched on her skin. She would try and mask her complexion under layers of makeup but the patches refused to hide and always manged to peek through the painted canvas.

On her wedding day, she concealed every spot on her face and arms with precision. My father walked in excited to see his new bride-to-be. He was aback by what he saw. He requested her to clean up and break through this unrealistic mask of painted beauty. He expressed deep feelings of love, told her that he loved her for who she is, and that she is truly beautiful without makeup. His loving words penetrated through her walls of self-rejection and right into her heart and soul in that tender moment. She wiped her face clean of society's unrealistic expectations of beauty, and reclaimed her authenticity.

That was the last day she ever hid her patches.

That may have been the last day she felt like it was the world against her.

That was the day she embraced herself.

Unrealistic beauty standards plague society like a disease. They are especially burdensome for women, who are conditioned to conform to these narrow ideals from a very young age. Beauty standards lack inclusivity – I am too dark, too fair, too thin, too fat, too curvy, too tall, too short, and so on. The list of "not being good enough" standards is endless.

This feeling of inadequacy when internalised can inflict deep damage upon mental health and self-image. It erodes self-esteem when stuck in a cycle of relentless judgement from self and others.

Our young girls now suffer because women adhere to these rules and endure the expectations rather than fighting them and embracing self-love. Adolescents today skip meals, purge, smoke, and shop compulsively in the process of trying to fill these voids that have been created by vultures preying on these standards of beauty.

These oppressive standards move from generation to generation and the cycle continues until we come in touch with our innate self-worth.

When we stop judging ourselves, we break the cycle.

When we heal, society heals. It begins to accept all races, colours, hairstyles, body shapes, body sizes and stretchmarks.

Everyone is enough in their own skin. All bodies are acceptable. And all women are worth pure self-love no matter their choices. Beauty standards need to be defined by the self, not society. We mustn't shy away from our perceived flaws because someone told us to. We may choose to do so, but only because it's a personal choice. Then we realise that we have always been perfect with or without correction.

When we get connected to our inner royalty, the world becomes our courtyard and a better place for our daughters – queens in the making.

So that they can accept themselves, their choices and shine and glow brighter, unabashed!

Magic happens when we accept ourselves

Lying flat on my back with complete surrender to our mother earth that holds us, I felt a strange sense of gratitude as I let all my weight go. I got reminded of the unconditional love and protection that we are showered with at every moment of our lives.

Suddenly, through my thoughts, my yoga trainer's soft gentle voice penetrated through: "Now take your attention to your fingers," she said. I was in the middle of a yoga practice called shavasana – taking my attention to each part of my body. Shavasana has the magical ability to mindfully bring one into the present moment. I found myself surrendering my fatigue, my aches, pains and my worries into the mother.

I brought my attention back from my thoughts to my fingers. But this time it was different. I felt like I was looking at my children's tender fingers. A familiar feeling of warmth took over. My heart was oozing with love, like that of a mother for a child. I had never acknowledged my little fingers before. I was so grateful. I finished class and made a conscious effort to look at my hands as my driver drove me back home. The back of my hands had popping veins, my skin had gone thin, they were dry and definitely more wrinkled than the last time I'd looked at them. I folded my fingers in and felt a subtle pain in the joints of my fingers indicating to me how much they do for me. Each line, each crease, each nail, and the skin on my hands had a story to tell. I further expanded my attention to my whole body and the revelation was heartbreaking. I severely take my body for granted. There's a sense of entitlement. Is there respect when there is entitlement? Will there really be loneliness when we acknowledge ourselves with kindness?

I tend to find myself lonely in a big crowd. I prefer not to have conversations to pass time and my internal response is to shut off. I often question this feeling of loneliness and my response to crowds. On observation, how can I feel a sense of belonging when I'm going through my life like an entitled oblivious queen where my own body is concerned?

My body feels lonely, disregarded, unwell and invalidated as it works for me all day from dawn to dusk with no break. Therefore, the aches and pains, the fatigue, the resistance, which then projects itself in my mind, leading to feelings of anxiety, sadness and overthinking. This, then, makes me feel terribly lonely and sometimes lost and confused in a crowd. Loneliness is a feeling whose balm is acceptance, love, inclusivity and communication. We all want to feel heard and understood. We all need reciprocation and our feelings validated, but we look for it externally. Do we take time out to nurture our body, mind and soul every single day of our lives? Do we look at our little fingers and toes and give ourselves a pat on our backs for pulling through every single day?

The experience lingered for days on end. I started viewing myself with so much tender love and care. I realised that I'm so relentless with my personal standards and it was my irrational belief of self-perfection that was isolating me and wounding my soul. It drove me to seek external validation, people-please, shrink my authentic self to fit in, because I had to be perfect. I had to perfectly eradicate that stammer, I had to perfectly eliminate every blemish on my skin, straighten every hair that had a curl, remove every roll of fat that came up on my body, kill every thought that begged to let go, rest and relax. I was far away from perfection and perfectly lonely.

My self-perception began to transform. I just needed a little more work and the intervention of divine grace to rain down on me.

Learning self-compassion

I had gone to my ashram in Bangalore, my home where my soul resides – the Art of Living International Centre. It was a five-day silence advanced meditation programme.

On day two, late in the evening during our last mediation of the day, I felt a warm comforting internal embrace – something I only knew theoretically but had never experienced before. There was a sudden pivotal shift within me. I instantly knew this was the profound intervention of liberating grace.

As this feeling took over me, I started to see a little girl, lonely, fearful, tired and pale, hiding within the warmth of this embrace. She was so alone and so scared with no hope of survival. As I looked into her eyes, I saw myself. Her eyes were full of pain, deeply sunken in – those eyes held all the trauma that came with the bullying, the fear of communication, the sexual abuse and the loneliness. Her eyes were layered with unsaid words, unexpressed emotions, and repressed actions. All the rejection not met with self-compassion till now. My eyes locked with her as time suspended. I saw clearly the intense agony my soul had absorbed while I was running away from her.

It was the fragmented part of my soul that I had abandoned

and left behind. She was alone and searching for belonging. She was the people-pleaser who based her worth on perfection and external validation.

I took her into my shelter and nurtured this part of me that I had cut away. I nursed her back to wholeness and then put her to rest. I grieved her passing but celebrated the reunion more. I became parent, child, and healing balm simultaneously. It was all within me right from the start.

Letting go of my limiting beliefs has helped me regain a hold on myself. A kind, gentle yet assertive hold. I regained autonomy over my life as a queen in control of the self and not a victim of the self. The sweet power that lies in this transition is what shifts the weight from victim to victor.

It has helped me slowly find my self-worth, set my boundaries, and embrace my dreams and desires with courage. I had to forgive myself, accept and heal my inner victim and then let her go.

And as a result, I have not only become a better person to myself but also a better counterpart in all my relationships.

Grace recalled my intrinsic power and that is true perfection.

I feel so fulfilled to look at the woman I am becoming today. My relationship with myself is evolving and my interpersonal relationships are becoming healthier.

Do I still love solitude? I do.

Do I love my interpersonal relationships? I most definitely do.

Do I love my relationship with faith? I could've never

done it without faith.

Do I love myself? More than anything in the world.

But the bigger question is, do I still feel lonely? On some days I do and I stand unafraid. I have learnt to give myself the space to fully feel everything I am feeling. Allow, accept, label and then use my tools to crawl out of that lonely place when I'm ready.

I am learning to rest in the safest place that I have – within MYSELF.

Loneliness is slowly becoming an epidemic and a health crisis. It is an unpleasant distressing emotional response to perceived isolation and helplessness. Loneliness is the cause of multiple physical and mental disorders. It is a complex feeling and is unique to each individual. One may feel lonely due to self-shame, disabilities, gossip and cancel culture, grief, retirement, changing jobs, schools, universities and cities, becoming a new parent and/or physical and mental-health problems. Each of them has a unique line of healthy coping skills. Hence, the modalities used would be made up of subjective and personalised approaches. If loneliness is affecting your wellbeing, there are multiple ways to get needed support.

Choose to break out and dance in the magic of self-love and self-acceptance, my dear. You can do it!

Diving into the self

1. How often do you find yourself feeling disconnected or isolated from others, and how do you typically respond to these emotions?

2. Can you recall the last time you experienced loneliness? What actions or thoughts helped you transition out of that state?

3. What are the most challenging aspects of loneliness for you, and why do you think they are particularly difficult?

4. What are the key distinctions between the feelings of loneliness and the experience of solitude?

5. What are some activities or hobbies that help you feel more connected to yourself or others?

6. When spending time alone, how do you discern between feelings of loneliness, isolation and abandonment versus opportunities for self-reflection, inner connection and personal development that solitude presents?

7. Do you think you might be affected by society's beauty standards or societal expectations and has it impacted your self-worth and confidence?

8. How do you think cultural or societal norms influence your experience of loneliness?

9. What are some ways you can communicate your feelings of loneliness to those close to you?

10. What strategies can you use to surround yourself with positive influences, engage in activities that affirm your self-worth, and create a narrative that you are whole and complete?

Loneliness is an empty void, seeking fulfilment through external connection. Yet, when transformed into solitude, it fosters the most profound bond – the one with the inner self.

Unveiling Childhood

The Heirloom of Trauma

I look into the mirror and see me. I recognise me, so familiar, but I also see a depth that makes me want to dive in. It is the gatekeeper of my soul, my inner child, my experiences, my feelings, my emotions and my past. I dive deeper and, through my freefall, I realise that I'm happy today. A happiness that didn't exist in me through my growing years. I was full of self-hate, volatility and shame. But I was too strong to admit it, so I played pretend.

As a mom of two, I meet my kids every morning, tell them I love them and send them off to school. I meet them post school, hug them, smother them, tell them I missed them and inquire about their day. If they had a good day, I congratulate them and if they fail, I remind them about the beauty of being human. If they cry, I tell them it's okay to cry and if I cry, I tell them my happiness isn't their responsibility. If I hurt them, I apologise and if I've been harsh or unreasonable I make up for it. I take a weekly review on my parenting skills and together we discuss the further line of parenting, highlighting our perfect imperfections and humanness.

My son struggled to play football and kept failing at his try-outs until one day he decided not to go and said it doesn't define his strength or popularity. My daughter is clear-headed and unapologetically herself.

My children are unafraid to express failure, disappointment, fragility, heartbreak or even their expectations to me. They are unafraid to admit their mistakes and do not fear retribution from me.

They are encouraging of my need to stay in my personal power and encourage my choices, personal, professional, financial, social or spiritual. We figure it all out, this way or that. I don't need to be perfect.

Is this even real? How did I get here? How did I find peace and happiness? How did I learn to be vulnerable and so forgiving of myself?

I broke pattern. I felt the feelings and I released the trauma. I flipped the irrational beliefs of unhealthy narratives and laid them down within diameters of humanness. My irrational beliefs of strength and perfection were broken down to bits.

These beliefs came from my childhood. My trauma surfaced from growing up in a household where everyone struggled with their personal battles. Every member of my family played pretend and projected happiness because vulnerability was dangerous. "I am strong" seemed to be the universal narrative in my household. Vulnerability and fragility were masked through strength and irrational assertion. My family environment instilled compassion, empathy and unbiased perspective but it also taught me that, "I have to be strong". My family accepted my failures but they were ruthless with themselves, "I must not fail". My mother had this innate urge to be perfect – the perfect mother, perfect wife, perfect daughter, perfect friend and perfect neighbour. Her struggle for perfection reflected in the myriad challenges that she may have faced every day. I watched closely, "I must be perfect", "I must please my man". I was afraid to express my inner feelings and review the adult behaviours in my home expecting rigid responses, "I must repress my feeling", "I must not have boundaries", "I must shy away from my own truth".

The self-worth of my family members hung on thin silk threads disguised through the projection of perfect self-confidence. My lack of self worth drove me into the hands of the perverted debauch for years.

This is the other side of my family. My comforting cosy casa also had an antithesis. They tried hard to be perfect and strong but maybe they tried too hard – almost rigid. My family was human after all. I wonder how many generations carried the heirloom of irrational strength, perfection, repression and patriarchy.

My life's journey has been a reflection of the irrational beliefs that stemmed from my home. I made choices to validate my confirmation bias. The psychological trauma that irrational beliefs of strength and perfection brought with them made its way into my relationships, my identity and my parenting journey, my first child being the victim of its ripple effect. I found myself going down the same path of strength, perfection and repression with my firstborn. When I realised my daughter was facing the cannonballs of my trauma, I decided to put a stop to it. I spent years trying to heal the wounds and undo the rigid knots of trauma that were tied to me. With my first baby's patience, kindness, resilience and support, my son received a healed version of me. And today, I put a stop to it. I ended this cycle of generational trauma. I let it go with forgiveness, love and gratitude for what it made me, all it taught me, and then it freed me.

Trauma inherited

Childhood trauma can occur when the child experiences overwhelming negative and unhealthy events that are emotionally painful or distressful. It is crucial that children undergoing trauma are provided with an emotionally and physically safe environment. The failure to provide children with support and safety can have lasting mental and physical effects. Children are very dependent and hence extremely vulnerable to trauma. Sensitivity and care are the cornerstones of a healthy childhood.

Childhood trauma can occur in many forms. Neglect, psychological, physical, or sexual abuse can lead to feelings of shame, guilt, diminished self-worth and sometimes even self-harm and suicidal tendencies. Children are usually susceptible to bullying and can be intimidated by community, school violence or even bullying by parents, teachers and caregivers. It is unfortunate that adult bullying towards children goes largely unnoticed. Adults may feel that being providers for the children entitles them to dominate and disrespect their children's boundaries. This sense of entitlement may not be vicious but simply lack of education and awareness on the part of the adult. This kind of callousness can cause hazardous feelings of rejection, exclusion, isolation, low self-esteem, impulsive anger outbursts and can even lead to depression and anxiety. Witnessing or experiencing domestic violence can damage the emotional health of a child leading to long-term attachment and trust issues.

Out of all the different forms of abuse, I believe, emotional abuse is the most damaging form of abuse. Manipulation and negative emotional messaging can lead to grave consequences. It is an invisible and misunderstood form of trauma that goes easily unnoticed. It comes with a sense of entitlement, dictatorship and manipulation that attacks the fragile, vulnerable child's mind. The growing child is yet to discover their authentic pure self. It is in the purity of this blank slate that the beautiful mind shifts into shape. It is unfortunate that this form of abuse is usually inflicted by the closest adults to the child and can easily condition the defenceless trusting mind to develop fearful and self-defeating beliefs.

Generational trauma

Often, the adults emotionally abusing children are themselves victims of generational trauma. Pain travels through families generation after generation, repeating destructive patterns until someone breaks the cycle. One needs to fully feel the pain to release it and this is when the cycle breaks. Both perpetrator and victim feel entitled to give and receive this mistreatment and endure the pain.

Children are expected to have higher emotional standards than their little minds can even fathom. They get held to unrealistic emotional expectations beyond their developmental capacity and are forced to cater to the unmet needs of the adult family members. The adults may not be comfortable accepting emotions in their children that they couldn't face in themselves. Due to this, children can start experiencing their age-appropriate feelings getting rejected. This rejection induces shame and poor self-acceptance that persists into adulthood.

Having had caregivers unable to be exemplary models of healthy self-regulation, these children enter adulthood lacking skills and coping tools to regulate difficult emotions and their nervous system themselves. Long-term, this manifests as emotional disconnect or suppression of discomfort.

It's important that these wounded children learn to accept, acknowledge and connect with their feelings without the generational pain and shame that preceded them. Through self-work, counselling therapy, meditation and support, they can learn to feel safe with their inner selves and discover a healing solitude that feels liberating rather than lonely and isolating.

Freedom emerges by releasing conditioned and deep-rooted projections and expectations that don't authentically belong to us. We uncover our deepest truth and our fragrant essence when we let go of who we're not. Breaking free of inherited trauma may be difficult but an exhilarating ride in the journey to wholeness.

Life presents both, wounds and the Shamanic wisdom to heal them.

Childhood trauma in adults often manifests as post-traumatic stress disorder (PTSD) or complex PTSD (C-PTSD). C-PTSD results from repeated trauma over time, while PTSD can stem from a single severe traumatic event. C-PTSD is a more severe form of PTSD.

In both, the limbic system gets flooded with stress hormones like adrenaline and cortisol. The brain gets stuck in fight-flight-freeze mode, with traumatic memories flashing over and over again along with associated emotions recurring involuntarily. One may feel like they are reliving the event in the present moment – giving rise to intense physical and emotional reactions like panic attacks, palpitations, irrational fears, anxiety, rapid heartbeat, etc.

With C-PTSD, one consistently feels on edge and unsafe with few or negligible coping mechanisms helping to manage emotions. While PTSD can ease over time, the trauma of C-PTSD gets physically embedded in the body, and professional care is needed.

One may feel consistently angry, guilty, afraid, ashamed, emotionally numb, hypersensitive or hypervigilant to threats. Destructive thought patterns can develop like "the world is dangerous", "I am unworthy" or "I'm unlovable", making us feel lonely and cut off from the world.

The feelings of isolation and disconnection get intensified. It may also lead to insomnia, eating disorders, anxiety disorders, depression or borderline personality, poor concentration and memory, irritability, and more.

Research confirms childhood trauma strongly correlates with adult mental-health struggles. Trauma impacts relationship skills and brain function. Studies overwhelmingly implicate childhood adversity in depression.

Healing happens by processing the stuck traumatic memories and associated triggers. Through therapy, the nervous system can be taught to regulate emotions again.

Childhood trauma creeps into adulthood: healing as an adult

Trauma, when unprocessed, finds its home in our body and stays in it as unconscious emotional wounds. It regularly manifests through outbursts, disconnection, and compromised physical health. For the healing process to occur, the trauma needs to be acknowledged and accepted; then the feelings can be felt when the natural emotions are allowed to flow. This release coupled with support will help us understand that trauma doesn't define us as human beings.

Feeling and releasing

It is very important to learn to feel our feelings. It is when we don't learn this basic skill that we start interpreting most of our difficult feelings as terrifying.

To heal trauma, we have to grieve. When we look at our grief as a friend who's come to release the pain and heal us, we can free ourselves from this trauma.

A step-by-step process that can help process childhood trauma with the help of a therapist can be extremely liberating.

Some tips are:

• Come into the present moment using grounding techniques.

• When grounded, go back to the event and try recalling every detail you remember with ease and conscious breathing.

• Now, pay attention to bodily sensations and emotions.

• Consciously identify and label emotions specifically.

• Allow yourself to fully feel and experience these.

• Share the experience with your mental-health practitioner and allow the support while you release these emotions and free yourself from this baggage.

• Love yourself and your humanness by giving yourself the tenderness and self-talk that your inner child needs to feel and hear.

Shifting from victim to victor – reframing the perspective

Traumatic experiences are like goldmines. They hold immense potential for growth and empowerment when we dig deep with resilience to seek the learning that lies inside. We can derive profound resilience from these mines of strength and resurrection as they break down into ashes only to survive and then rise like a phoenix. Many highly accomplished people have reframed their narratives and channelled trauma into fuel for future success.

The stories we tell ourselves and the meaning we assign to the trauma are the keys in determining whether we move forward or stay powerless and stagnant. We all have the capacity to consciously direct our trauma responses to serve our growth and expand our wisdom. The victor shines through when we reset and redirect the unproductive emotional responses of our victim mentalities rather than dismissing or indulging them.

Our perspective, interpretations and choices belong to us. It is by taking ownership of our thoughts, behaviours and actions that we transcend our trauma into evolution, empowerment and wisdom. All suffering holds the potential to shape-shift and morph into limitless possibilities of growth and expansion. Once we release our self-limiting beliefs, we cannot be defeated by destiny's blows.

These storms adorn the age-old teachings of fortitude, self-mastery, faith, surrender, forgiveness and gratitude. When we imbibe these attributes and hard-won gifts, we become forces to be reckoned with.

Where I come from does not confine where I can go. What I learnt doesn't define what I do, and what I was taught doesn't define who I am. I SIMPLY AM – UNTOUCHED, UNADULTRATED, PURE.

Diving within the self

1. What new tools or strategies could you explore to end the cycle of generational trauma and regulate yourself in a healthier way?

2. Did any memories come to mind as you read this

chapter?

3. What emotions did these memories evoke in you?

4. Do you feel powerless or confined by these memories and emotions?

5. How can you recognise and validate these memories and feelings in a healthy way?

6. What steps can you take to release yourself from the burden of these emotions?

7. How have your childhood experiences influenced your thoughts, beliefs, and behaviours as an adult?

8. In what ways have your childhood experiences impacted your relationships and the choices you make in them?

9. What coping mechanisms have you developed to manage past trauma, and are they still serving you well?

10. What new tools or strategies can you explore to break the cycle of generational trauma and promote healthier self-regulation?

11. What steps can you take to embrace your past as a part of your story without letting it define your future?

Human Bonds

Cruising Through the Layers of Relationships

I got married when I was in my very early 20s. I was already financial independent from the time I became a successful model at the age of 17. But I gave up my financial autonomy and everything I had built when I got married.

I contorted myself to fit rigid expectations in my new role, some preconditioned and some self-imposed. My fear of rejection demanded that I completely and fully alter myself. I gave up my career, gave up my friends and changed the way I dressed, the way I spoke and even tried to change the way I thought. Everything in my life became about how I can fit in, how to impress my new family, feel accepted and become the perfect daughter-in-law and perfect wife.

Losing myself in the complex maze of perfection

But the more I twisted trying to shape-shift into perfection, the further away I went from myself. I completely lost myself in the complex maze of inauthenticity that I was building with my own hands. I became estranged from my own essence and my needs. The wider the gap within myself, the more my worth diminished. It remained determined by external validation, hooking itself onto others' approval. I never really received the validation I was looking for, in the format I hoped for. I developed more resentment, more entitlement, self-rejection, and total loss of self-confidence. This cycle continued for years on loop.

I struggled with my sense of self and may have suppressed a large part of me in the process of my eager need to adapt. The foundation of our relationship crumbled under the weight of external expectations and inner turmoil.

In the earlier phase of my marriage, I was focused on myself, which came from a space of emptiness, resentment, expectation, validation, helplessness and entitlement. Today I focus on myself too, but from a space of fullness, self-acceptance, unconditional love, focus, and goals. The difference is night and day. I previously grasped on to loose twigs of fleeting validation; now I hold on to myself with anchored strength, and self-care emanates from a feeling of integrity.

Our marriage has now shaped into a solid companionship that took a unique form of unconditional support and care when we decided to break out of the conforming chains that were choking us.

Are we really entitled?

I realised I was co-creating my reality by viewing my life through my narrow lens and then choosing to respond in a way suitable to me. By accepting that I played a role in each dynamic that caused me pain, I experienced a sense of freedom in my marriage rather than blaming or playing the victim. This, I discovered, is also one of the truest forms of empathy both for the self and the other.

When we react out of emptiness and unmet needs, we reject parts of ourselves. It blinds us from asking a very primal question, "How did I create this suffering?"

At the end of it, once I took accountability for my wounds, my worth, my happiness and my life, clarity emerged.

I learnt that I am not entitled. Entitlement can be a dangerous self-harming weapon while we carry on assuming the world owes us.

Entitlement steals away happiness, empathy and compassion. It builds disappointment, frustration, helplessness and heartbreak.

We cannot be admired and respected if we don't admire and respect ourselves. Self-love is the basis of a strong foundation in any relationship. It helps us set our own boundaries and respect others' boundaries and switch from unhealthy co-dependencies to healthy interdependencies.

Understanding companionship and intimate connections

Earlier I believed that companionship only lies in an intimate partnership and my marriage endured the pressure of this belief. Today my definition of companionship has changed.

Every person who is important to me and belongs to my core circle of relationships are my companions.

My girlfriends form the bedrock of this core circle of relationships – our sisterhood is a sanctuary for me without judgement. They have been my voice of reason, my shoulders to cry on, my cheerleaders and my private safe space, where I can reveal my vulnerability and my strength.

They play a vital role in giving me the courage to roar and, when I feel most alone, they await to welcome me back home with hugs, laughter, and tears once I reach out a hand from isolating darkness.

Expectations – healthy or not?

Expectations ride most relationships, for better or worse; they can be both healthy and unhealthy. Our healthy expectations help us set our boundaries and our unhealthy expectations help us understand our triggers and fears.

Expecting perfection in our partner and expecting them to change their values and be the only source of providing happiness and companionship to us burdens the relationship. This pressure of unhealthy co-dependency can lead to conflict and endless, pointless arguments.

Relationships cannot be devoid of expectations. We all

have our negotiable and non-negotiable needs. It is important for us to be clued into ourselves and set healthy standards of happiness from the self and the other. The key for the distinction between healthy and unhealthy expectations in relationships is distinguishing between our needs and fears, co-dependence and interdependence.

There are many times when we feel our expectations are not met. I have felt it multiple times in my life. As I dug deeper, I found that the disappointment came from learnt beliefs that we gather over the course of our lives – what we think will make us happy, what we think should make us happy.

The answers lie at a deeper level. Our triggers are arrows that point to the depths of our being. When we get triggered and take our focus within, we will find our needs; we will find parts of us that need to be healed and we will find our authentic selves.

Is my expectation coming from empowering aspirations (our needs in a relationship) or limiting beliefs (our fears) projected on to my partner?

Once we identify our needs versus fears, we develop clarity. It helps us understand and communicate our expectations better, even if it is support through our fears and fragility that we need. This gentle approach creates a safe platform for healthy dialogue and working together as a couple or partners.

Simple steps go a long way, like compliments, expressing appreciation and acknowledgement of the work done by the partner towards fulfilment of expectations, compassionate and respectful conflict resolution, being considerate and empathetic when expressing concerns, and steering clear of nagging. Working towards actively understanding each other's emotional, mental and body language creates an understanding about each other that is loving and intuitive.

Multiple companions for life

I believed that the rights of companionship were only with the intimate partner. This landed up putting a truckload of weight on my marriage. With passing time, my understanding about companionship evolved.

My core circle of relationships are also my companions. These relationships anchor me and create a space of protection for me. I cannot even imagine how life may have been if not for my girlfriends. My women friends have been no less than true companions, in the most authentic way. They cocoon me in their warm hugs, open their ears when I need to be heard, open their hearts and love me deeply with shared laughter and tears. They provide me with unconditional acceptance and are a great source of strength.

All my companions have helped mould me into who I am and who I'm becoming. We dig our hands in wet mud as we help mould each other in discovering the best versions of ourselves.

One lifetime in itself is too short to experience love wholly. Yet we choose to spend our time in anger, resentment and fear. Self-love has the most fragrant essence that makes love fully blossom.

It is through the cracks of the broken heart that the light

shines. Fear not the relationship with yourself because that is where the heart of all your relationships is born.

Diving within the self

1. What are some ways you can continue to pursue your own interests, goals, and passions?

2. Are you able to balance nurturing your partnership while also pursuing your passions?

3. Make a list of your expectations in your relationship.

4. Categorise these expectations into negotiables, non-negotiables, co-dependent, and interdependent.

5. How do your expectations influence the dynamics of your relationship?

6. How can you foster open and honest communication with your partner about your needs, desires, and expectations, creating a safe space for two-way dialogue?

7. In what ways can you prioritise self-love and a feeling of wholeness while maintaining healthy emotional interdependence within your marriage?

8. What steps can you take to ensure your personal growth aligns with the growth of your relationship?

9. How can you create rituals or habits that reinforce the bond between you and your partner?

10. What role does mutual respect play in your relationship, and how can it be cultivated?

Gloriously Grateful

A Heart Full of Joy

One night, I was lying on the grass under the pitch-black night sky staring into the infinite expanse of the darkness. Suddenly I found myself gripped by primal fears - of the rustling insects and the endless darkness. I began to fear my mortality as obscure thoughts about death took over my mind-space and then profound loneliness. Anxiety quickened my heart rate and almost stopped my breath. I jumped upright, desperate to escape the silent vastness surrounding me, and decided to bolt to my room.

It was the last full moon of 2023 and I was blessed to have made it to my ashram for a meditation programme where I could end the year in silence and reconnect with myself.

In my panic, I nearly abandoned my sacred promise – to slow down and move gently through these five days in the ashram. Honouring my body, mind and soul with nurturing love, respect and slowness after a gruelling year, I decided to consciously walk slowly, eat with mindfulness, brush my teeth with awareness, and even watch my thoughts with detachment and disconnect. But the moonlit wilderness awakened old terrors within me. The fear seemed unsurmountable and life threatening. I longed for the safety of the four walls of my room.

As I scrambled pieces of myself together and made it up to run for dear life, something stopped me in my tracks – the magnificent golden moon, fearlessly spilling her expansive light across the sky. So quiet yet so majestic, she stared down with comforting light that befriended the darkness. Surrounding her, a tapestry of silver stars beamed confidently. Not dimming their glitter for the darkness nor diminishing from the expanse – simply owning their glory, unabashed and true to themselves.

I stood still, awestruck like an innocent child, as the heavenly lights bathed me. My fears began to melt away and I lay back down. Never had I witnessed such beauty – the moon so boldly luminous, the stars glittering like crystals and the blackness of the velvet sky, royal and deep.

Even if the moon and stars shone brighter or the night's depth darker, I felt like I could trust my own inner fires to sustain me. My inner fire ignited, I inhaled deeply and exhaled slowly, realigning with my highest self and connecting to the messages glimmering down upon me.

The ashram was silent, my mind was silent and my body was still. There was no longing for anyone or anything, nowhere to rush to and nothing to do and no fear of living or dying… all I was absorbed in was the present moment. Suspended in a vacuum of nothingness, my thoughts dissipated.

The vacuum of nothingness

If we look at it closely, what does the present moment really hold?

It holds nothing, no time, no feelings, no attachment; all it has is the profound connection to oneself. I took a deep breath in while I absorbed my experience. I felt compelled to hold my breath for a few seconds. At that moment all thoughts vanished and I fully experienced the present moment.

My experience was validated for me, through me and to me.

This epiphany, this surreal experience of the SELF in the PRESENT moment under the stars has been etched into my soul. I am not sure how long I lay there in wonder and watched the beauty in the silence that enchanted me.

My experience stayed with me all night and the next day, and my heart filled up with gratitude. How could I have had such an ecstatic experience on my own, alone in the silence with no intoxications or any external factors? I also realised that it was the magnitude of gratitude that beat my fear. I walked back to my room, slowly and fearlessly in complete surrender, and slept like a baby tucked within the blanket of grace, love and protection that night.

It was the silent mind that was able to acknowledge the

beauty that was being bestowed upon it, and to surrender to the present moment. It was faith that fuelled my gratitude and 2024 was a beautiful beginning to a reconstructed me. The experience on the night of 28th of December 2023 still lights up my heart like that golden moon and those sparkly silver stars.

The power of solitude consistently baffles me. It is jewelled with stillness and an ethereal presence that never fails to eventually reveal such magnanimous splendour. No substances or fanfare are required – just a mind quiet enough to receive the abundant gifts it holds.

Gratitude is like those stars and moon in a night sky. Either we can look at the darkness and allow it to take over us, making us run, hide, and live in despair, anger, resentment, or we can look at the stars, moon, shooting stars and all the beauty the night sky offers us along with the darkness.

Today, I accept both the darkness and the golden moon that my life has to offer. I am terribly afraid of the darkness on some days but I don't forget to latch on to the light that the night sky has to offer as well. For it is fear that teaches surrender.

My life has been turbulent, but it is a turbulent journey that gives greater joy on touching the runway safely.

I am able to now see how darkness and light, fear and surrender, despair and hope can coexist within me. The ambivalent beauty of who we are.

For it is only fear that eventually teaches you to surrender.

Gratitude – transcending into grace

Gratitude is one of the healthiest and most powerful coping mechanisms when in distress. It takes you from the micro temporary unhealthy emotional state to a macro healthy perspective. It is the best friend to our SUPERPOWER of PERSPECTIVE.

This shift from micro to macro occurs through appreciating what IS instead of fixating on what is not. The macro holds the blessings that already surround us – the wonders that flow freely and light up our lives. All we have to do is pause and notice.

Consciously practising gratitude helps us transcend from a state of feeling grateful to abiding in a grateful state of being. It evolves from conscious practice to unconscious perspective.

A beautiful book, laughter with a friend, the cosy couch to rest in, the wind in my hair, the sound of children playing in the park below my room, the perfume I spray on, the smile of my children, the support of my partner, the smell of my dogs, my beating heart, the setting sun, the rising moon – all beautiful things to behold if only you pause for a bit and allow the joy to seep in.

This state of being acts like a magnet.

Gratitude attracts GRACE, abundance, happiness.

As you become more grateful, life will give you more things to be grateful for.

Reframing the narrative – embracing the lessons

It's easy to be grateful for the good things in life. But

am I thankful for the brutal bullying that came with my stammering as a kid?

The sexual predator?

My daughter's scoliosis?

My struggle with having my second baby and the surrogacy?

Losing my mother to the brutal ravage of cancer?

And so on…

It's taken me years of inner-child work to reframe these painful experiences. I like to call them my negative positive experiences. The experiences are negative only on paper today because they have lost their emotional charge. I am grateful for the gifts that they have given me.

My troubled childhood taught me that I am beyond all limitations and capable of achieving my dreams and that all problems have a solution.

The sexual predator taught me to love and respect my body because it is sacred and divine. I learnt to set and respect my boundaries and that today I will never be a victim to anyone again and these boundaries translate into all areas of my life.

My daughter's scoliosis taught me that, sometimes in life, surrender is the only way forward. There is no love like that of parent. Watching my daughter live with a deformity and then go into that eight-hour corrective surgery taught me that the only option I had was to let go.

My son's surrogacy reaffirmed to me the changing nature of life. I carried one baby and I couldn't carry the other. Embracing change and flowing with the tide keep body, mind, and soul at peace.

Losing my mother to cancer and watching her journey through it taught me resilience. The grace and surrender through which she went through her struggles showed me how powerful the mind can be. She had this innate ability to be hopeful and grateful for all she had.

This is a lesson I will take to my grave. It also showed me my own capabilities and helped me discover my own strength as a woman.

Would I have opted for less pain and suffering in my journey?

Most definitely yes but then again, that's not in my control.

What is in my control is how I view them, how I respond to them and what I learn through the ride.

I remember reading this somewhere and it helped me so deeply:

Anything that annoys you is teaching you patience.

Anyone that abandons you is teaching you how to stand up on your own two feet.

Anything that angers you is teaching you forgiveness and compassion.

Anything that has power over you is teaching you how to take your power back.

Anything you hate is teaching you unconditional love.

Anything you fear is teaching you courage to overcome your fear.

Anything you cannot control is teaching you how to let go.

This wisdom resonated profoundly within me. Each bout of suffering can transform from painful anguish into targeted training for growth and self-discovery.

I bow in respect with open palms as I accept the invitation to surrender.

It may have never been mine to clutch so tightly anyhow.

Gratitude, the mother of abundance

I met my spiritual master, Gurudev Sri Sri Ravi Shankar, some time ago. As I watched him share his pearls of wisdom, filling the amphitheatre in the ashram with fun and laughter, I seemed to be the only one among thousands crying that day.

I looked around the ashram, seeing so many thousands of people, sometimes lakhs, finding their home and peace under his wing. He's like a father and mother to us all.

So why the tears that day? As I watched him speak, my heart swelled with sadness as I realised that until then all I ever did was ask from the divine – for peace, strength, things, everything I wanted, even if merely a pin. I cried realising I'd received everything I asked for.

I decided never to ask for anything again. I wanted to live in surrender and allow the divine to do whatever was meant for me, receiving the abundant grace and protection that comes with that. I decided I wanted to live in gratitude, working to better myself, loved ones, community, and environment – using my strengths to focus on macro goals instead of getting sucked into potholes.

As these thoughts ran through my head, my entire being became gratitude. My goals grew clearer, the path opening in my mind and thereafter manifesting outwardly too.

I learnt to chase my goals with focus, ambition, passion but also with peace, faith and surrender. I learnt to abundantly enjoy the flow on the way to my destination.

Gratitude is the mother of abundance.

Blossoming through gratitude

Gratitude fuels self-esteem. Gratitude is the core value of self-confidence. It teaches us to celebrate rather than critique. Genuinely giving thanks makes life more beautiful and is the antidote to the corruption that lies within entitlement and taking goodness for granted.

Even amidst trials that shadow gratitude like an eclipse, there is always some blessing to be thankful for. Little blessings are the silver lining behind every cloud – we just have to look. And while we do that, we can thank the universe for the air that we breathe, our heart that beats, the eyes that see, care for a loved one or even the wise lessons that come hand-in-hand with our pain.

Appreciation and gratitude give birth to hope, happiness and optimism.

Support replaces antagonising.

Calm replaces anxiety.

Wisdom replaces fear.

Confidence replaces doubt.

We are able to develop a knowing that we will come to light. With a belief in our inner resources that we will not just remain alive but we will thrive, blossom, bloom and shine even through the storm.

When we jump into a river and go with the flow, we will see that it supports us. There is rhythm to everything in life. We just have to catch the note and sing along.

So, I sing along.

I am so grateful to be right here… right now… right where I need to be.

"Every breath I take, I breathe in trust, and every breath I release, I breathe out conscious gratitude."

There is joy intrinsic to being that is not there in doing.

Diving into the self

1. List 10 things, people, and experiences for which you feel genuinely grateful.

2. Make a list of five things, people and experiences you are grateful for even amidst challenges or difficulties.

3. Do you believe that gratitude has the power to create a more positive and resilient mindset?

4. How can you harness gratitude as a tool to shift your narrative during times of hardship, stress, or feelings of scarcity?

5. What hidden gifts or lessons have you learnt from past hardships?

6. In what ways can gratitude help you transcend through fear?

7. What are some methods you can use to regularly practise gratitude, such as keeping a gratitude journal, sharing your appreciation with others, or engaging in thankfulness

meditation?

8. How can you transform your perspective from one of scarcity and lack to one of abundance and blessings?

9. Do you believe that gratitude can help you recognise the opportunities available to you? If so, how can you apply this in your life?

10. How has gratitude influenced your relationships with others?

11. How can you incorporate gratitude into your daily routine to enhance your life experience?

12. What are some obstacles that may prevent you from practising gratitude, and how can you overcome them?

Story (Part 2)

That blessed night, while wandering in the enchanted forest, under the magnificent oak tree, her life changed. The mysterious mystic brought out the magic in her that had always existed. His long beard flowed like a river, and his hair danced with the wind, but it was the sparkle in his eyes that captivated her. His beguiling voice that had the depth of the ocean in it lifted the burdens off her heart.

The once vibrant light in her eyes that had faded and dimmed to a muted grey was finding its glow again.

With a graceful wave of his hand, the mystic conjured an image before her. He showed her a young girl, her eyes brimming with tears, ensnared by thick, dark bands that coiled around her like a serpent. To her astonishment, the princess realised that these bands were born from her own mind and stemmed from her very thoughts.

"Your voice," the mystic said to her gently, "is like this young girl. She does not realise that she is the one who binds herself. The serpent is your friend pointing right to your bondage. Within you lies a voice as unique and powerful as the stars themselves, waiting to be unleashed. Believe in its beauty. You have the power to unbind the chains, and let your spirit shine as bright as the dawn. Release it, and true freedom will follow."

As the vision faded, so did the mystic, leaving the princess alone beneath the silver moon and the glimmering stars. He had disappeared but left a part of him with her that kept her whole and unbroken. She had felt different – lighter, as if a burden had been lifted. She found herself laughing and weeping beneath the heavens, transformed by the revelation.

With newfound strength, the magical book in her hand and her head held high, the princess returned to the palace. The following day, the courtiers were struck speechless as the princess spoke with clarity and confidence, sharing her vision of a kingdom founded on justice, equality, inclusivity and compassion – a land where all were welcomed, regardless of their differences. Her radiance left them awestruck.

In a grand ceremony witnessed by the entire kingdom, the king and queen honoured their daughter's journey of wisdom and self-discovery. They placed a crown upon her head, a symbol of her future reign. "I crown the princess," declared the king, "not only for her compassion towards all beings but for her courage to fight her fears and embrace her true self. May this crown serve as a reminder that your true power comes from within."

And the princess smiled, knowing she would carry this truth in her heart till kingdom come.

She plucked the crown off her head and held it to her heart because she knew a profound truth that royalty comes from within.

And inner royalty can never be cancelled.

"And that, your highness,

you are majestic – YOU ARE ROYAL.

Shine bright, shine free."

Afterword

When I first heard about Sohini's memoir, I was immediately drawn to it. As someone who has been an introvert my entire life and has been vocal about the importance of finding one's inner self, her journey resonated with me on a profound level.

As I immersed myself in the pages of this memoir, I was struck by Sohini's raw honesty and unwavering vulnerability. She fearlessly confronts the pain of her past and the challenges she encountered along the way, inspiring readers to embrace their own struggles with the same courage and determination.

Throughout my own journey, I have found solace and strength through introspection and faith, much like Sohini. Her words serve as a powerful reminder that we all have the capacity for growth and transformation, even in the face of adversity.

For within every struggle lies an opportunity for growth, and within every individual lies the potential for greatness.

In a world that often celebrates the loud and the bold, Sohini's story, "Cancelled to Crowned" is a powerful reminder of the strength and beauty that can be found in the quiet moments of introspection.

May her words inspire you to embrace your own journey, to find your inner voice, and to never stop seeking the truth that lies within.

Samir Soni